MW01247548

IT IS NOT WHERE YOU STARTED,

it's where you

FINISHED

HEZEKIAH BROWN PHD

It Is Not Where You Started, It's Where You Finished
Copyright © 2024 by Hezekiah Brown PhD

ISBN: 9798894790077 (sc)
ISBN: 9798894790190 (hc)
ISBN: 9798894790084 (e)

The Reading Glass Books
1-888-420-3050
www.readingglassbooks.com
fulfillment@readingglassbooks.com

TABLE OF CONTENTS

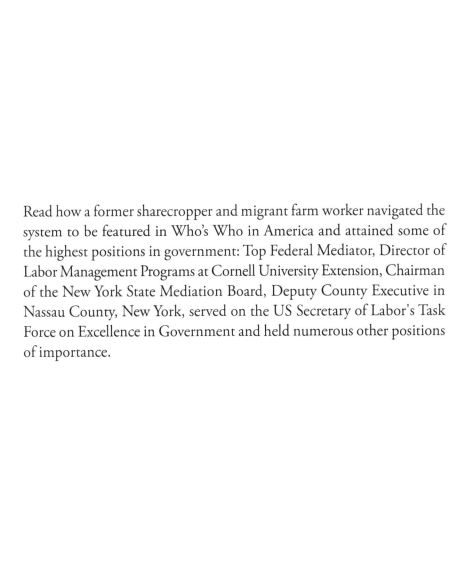

Read how a former sharecropper and migrant farm worker navigated the system to be featured in Who's Who in America and attained some of the highest positions in government: Top Federal Mediator, Director of Labor Management Programs at Cornell University Extension, Chairman of the New York State Mediation Board, Deputy County Executive in Nassau County, New York, served on the US Secretary of Labor's Task Force on Excellence in Government and held numerous other positions of importance.

This book is written in memory of our Granddaughter:

Chanee Monique Brown (1988-2006)

May her soul rest in peace.

AUTOBIOGRAPHY
OF
HEZEKIAH "SONNY" BROWN

IT IS NOT WHERE YOU STARTED, IT'S WHERE YOU FINISHED.

HEZEKIAH BROWN, PHD

ABOUT THE AUTHOR

Hezekiah Brown
Arbitrator-Mediator

In 2003, Hezekiah Brown retired from his position as Deputy County Executive of Nassau County and moved to Elizabeth City, North Carolina.

He served as a member of the Board of Visitors at Elizabeth City State University, Member of the Elizabeth City-Pasquotank County Community Relations Commission and served on the Pasquotank County Planning Board.

 He is a Veteran Arbitrator and Mediator who has developed his skills in the Corporate and Labor Relations field for more than 50 years. He is currently one of the foremost authorities in this profession. His expertise is regularly being sought by top Administrators on the State and National level as well as academia's.

His is the former Director of Labor-Management programs at Cornell University where he taught arbitration, mediation, collective bargaining, contract administration managing conflict, anger management, problem solving, team building, change management, diversity. In addition, he wrote the curriculum for Cornell University Extension Dispute Resolution Certificate Program which attracted students from such counties as Saudi Arabia, Cypress, Italy, Bangladesh, South America, and Australia.

Hezekiah's other expertise is in conflict resolution, employment discrimination and joint labor-management training. He has worked in the Industrial and Labor Relations field for over 50 years serving as a negotiator for labor and management and served for 12 years as a Federal Mediator. In addition, he served as the Chief Mediator and Chairman of the New York State Mediation Board and a member of the Mario Cuomo Cabinet.

Hezekiah has mediated and arbitrated over 5000 Labor-Management and Community disputes in the United States including the Virgin Islands and Puerto Rico.

In 1992, he was selected as one of the ten instructors to visit Russia to teach Contract Administration and conflict resolution as they embarked on making the transition to the market economy.

In 1995, he was again selected as one of ten instructors to travel to Europe to study the Global application of Cooperation between Labor and management. Upon his return from Europe, he was selected by United States Secretary of Labor, Robert Reich to serve on the Labor-Management Task Force for excellence in State and Local Government. After the work done by the Task Force, the recommendations were unanimously accepted by the United States Congress.

He has received numerous awards and recognitions for his work as a professional and Community Leader:

- Presidential Recognition Award for Community Service awarded by President Ronald Reagan

- The Federal Mediation and Conciliation Service Director's Award

- Black Achiever in Industry

- Martin Luther King Humanitarian

- Queens College Public Servant of the Year

- NAACP Community Service and Education

- Hofstra University Unispan Award

- Links Incorporated: Award of Appreciation Outstanding Public Service and Professional Achievement

Hezekiah has been recognized by the Key Women of America; The Suffolk County Black Bar Association' The University of Bridgeport; National Association of Black School Educators; The Incorporated Village of Hempstead; The Tow of Hempstead; Nassau County and the State of New York.

In 1999, Hezekiah was elected to the Board of Trustees for the Incorporated Village of Hempstead, New York and ran for Mayor in 2001. He served on the Hempstead Board of Education.

In May of 2008, he was inducted into the Prestigious National Academy of Arbitrators.

Hezekiah received a Bachelor of Science Degree from State University of New York, Empire State College and was awarded an Honorary PhD. From Cornell University Extension.

Mr. Brown continued his community service in Elizabeth City, North Carolina and was awarded the AAPR Legend of the Year Award, Links Incorporated Public Service and Professional Achievement award, Lenora Jarvis-Mackey Award for Outstanding Commitment to Excellence in the community.

He currently serves on the Elizabeth City/Pasquotank County Community Relations Commission, Vice-President of the Local Chapter of AARP, member of the Pasquotank County Planning Board, and Chairman of the Hope Group and serves as Chairman of the 20/20 Vision Committee, Celebration Our Diversity. Hezekiah serves as a volunteer with the River City Youth Program.

He has been married to Zelma Christine Brown for 64 years and they are the proud parents of Rodney L. Brown and Chandra D. Brown-King, and two granddaughters, Crystal Nicole Brown and Chanee (deceased).

Hezekiah is an active member of Mt. Lebanon AME Zion Church.

In 1957, while serving as a US Army Paratrooper in the 101st Airborne Division (327 Airborne Battle Group), the Specialist Brown deployed to Little Rock, Arkansas to help enforce the desegregation of Little Rock Central High School.

FIRST AFRICAN AMERICAN TO SERVE IN KEY POSITIONS

Hezekiah Brown has been the first in numerous instances. He has worked at every level of government including serving as CEO of a family-owned and operated conflict resolution consulting business. He has held high-level positions at the city, village, town, county, state and federal government levels including serving on the Hempstead Board of Education, elected to village government and ran for mayor of the Incorporated Village of Hempstead.

He was the first African-American to serve as:

- Chairman of the New York State Mediation Board

- New York State Employment Relations Board

- President of the Long Island Industrial Relations Research Association

- First African-American to serve as a peacemaker to keep labor-management peace during the Democratic Convention when Bill Clinton was nominated as the Democratic Presidential Candidate

- First African-American to serve as Chairman of the town of Hempstead Public Employment Relations Board

- First African-American to serve as director of labor-management programs at Cornell University extension.

- First African-American to serve as impartial Chairman for the League of Voluntary Hospitals covering 180,000 employees

- Served as impartial chairman for the Association of Private Hospitals

- First African-American to serve as Project Director for a Minority Arbitrator training program

- Served as Deputy Labor Czar for the Jacob Javits Convention Center.

- The 10th African-American selected to serve as a Commissioner with the Federal Mediation & Conciliation Service.

- Member of the prestigious National Academy of Arbitrators

Played a significant role in electing the:

- First African-American Judge in the City of Buffalo, New York

- First African-American New York State Assemblyman in the City of Buffalo, New York

- First African-American Mayor in Long Island and New York City.

- First African-American to the Nassau County Legislature

- First African-American elected state-wide in New York State

- First African-American to serve as Democratic Deputy Nassau County Executive

Finally, the 327 airborne battle group was the first company to arrive in Little Rock Arkansas to enforce the Brown vs the Board of Education Supreme Court decision which ultimately ended segregated schools in the South.

- Author of two books:
  - All Type Of Conflict Can Be Resolved and
  - A Case For Reparation

- He has arbitrated and mediated over 5,000 labor-management and community disputes

- Travelled to Russia and other parts of Europe to study the application and appreciation of Employee and Management Relations.

- Upon his retirement, he received an honorary Ph.D. from Cornell University extension in New York City.

- Appeared in *Who's Who* in America in 2023.

- In 2022, he celebrated 50 years as a Professional Neutral and received a Presidential Community Service Award from President Ronald Regan

MARQUIS
Who'sWho®
Since 1898

Hezekiah Brown featured in Who's Who in America in 2023!

Celebrating 50 years as a professional neutral, Arbitrator, Mediator, Educator, Entrepreneur and Author.

Hez has resolved over five thousand labor-management, and community disputes and traveled to Russia, Europe, the Virgin Islands and successfully resolved disputes at the United Nations.

As a result of his outstanding professional career, he will be listed in Marquis Who's Who in America in 2023.

Confirmation letter:

Dear Hezekiah Brown,

Congratulations on your inclusion as a Marquis Who's Who biographical listee! In order to recognize your distinction appropriately, we will feature you in our flagship hardcover registry, Who's Who in America.

Marquis Who's Who has been the world's preeminent biographer since 1899. Each year we strive to continue the tradition established by our founder, Albert Nelson Marquis, over 120 years ago with the first publication of Who's Who in America. That mission is to profile those individuals who have made a difference by virtue of the positions of responsibility they hold and/or due to noteworthy accomplishments they have made.

I would like to congratulate you on the accomplishments that have captured the attention of the Marquis Who's Who Selection Committee. We are honored to recognize you among others in your specialized field and within the Marquis Who's Who organization and wish you all the best in your future endeavors.

Sincerely,

The Marquis Who's Who Editorial Team

Hezekiah Brown with Bill Clinton

HEZEKIAH "SONNY" BROWN CELEBRATING 50 YEARS AS A PEACEMAKER AND COMMUNITY ACTIVIST

Hez recently celebrated 50 years as a professional neutral. He has successfully arbitrated and mediated over 5000 labor-management and community disputes. He is a member of the prestigious National Academy of Arbitrators and served as a member of Governor Mario Cuomo Cabinet. He has the unique distinction of successfully mediating a labor- management dispute at the United Nations.

Hezekiah Brown with former Governor Mario Cuomo

He has served at every level of Government, Federal Mediator, Chairman of the New York State Mediation Board, Chairman of the Town of Hempstead Public Employment Relation Board, Deputy County Executive of Nassau County, and Elected to The Hempstead Board of Trustees, Hempstead Board of Education and unsuccessfully ran for Mayor.

REMARKS BY GOVERNOR MARIO M. CUOMO
HEZEKIAH BROWN'S FUNDRAISER

THURSDAY, FEBRUARY 22, 2001
NASSAU HOTEL AND CONVENTION CENTER

Someone said on the way in "I'm surprised to see you here, Governor. Why would you come all the way to Hempstead to a fundraiser?"

I guess one good reason is enough, and that's Hezekiah Brown. I have known him for some time. I became familiar with his unusual talents and his splendid character when he worked with me in Albany. I discovered then he was an extremely well-educated man, and that he's smart too, which is, of course, something beyond being "educated."

He was the State's leading mediator, which meant that he had good judgment and was persuasive as an individual.

But he was also a former paratrooper, which meant he was tough.

I learned he was married to a beautiful woman with two children. He's had two granddaughters since then, something which makes him really special as far as I'm concerned.

Then recently I discovered that Hezekiah was about to add another credential to his extraordinary resume: he was going to run for the office of Mayor of the Village of Hempstead.

Frankly, I was delighted. There's nothing this country needs more than good people in politics and Hezekiah Brown is a good people.

I'm glad he chose Hempstead as the place to live and start his political career because his becoming Mayor here will benefit all the residents of this important part of the State... and will also be a tremendous boost to Democrats.

His victory would inspire Democrats in Nassau County and go on to greater victories here in the County in the fall and then next year at the State level.

Let's remember, Hempstead is no ordinary village. Hempstead is larger than the two cities in Nassau: Long Beach and Glen Cove.

As a matter of fact, Hezekiah Brown is absolutely right when he says Hempstead itself should be a city! It has its own police force, sanitation department and other services and it has the population. If it were a city, it would get a million-and-a-half dollars in revenue sharing. As of now you probably know, it only gets fifteen thousand.

Hez is making sure that his run helps the Democrat by running not as part of the "ABC" party, or the "Progress" Party, or the "Unity" Party, or the "Disunity" party, he's running as a Democrat because that's what he is and frankly that's what most people in Hempstead are... maybe by ten-to-one.

And he will win... if those of us who support him do the right thing for the next three weeks.

What's the right thing? Locate every voter you can find and I suggest you concentrate on voters, people who do vote, and will vote again, not just people who can vote but regularly ignore the opportunity. Get those prime voters, shake their hand, look them in the eye and say "Hez Brown is a good man." "He's smart, he's tough and he's right!" "He's going to make us a city and make us better."

And incidentally, if you can write a check to "Democrats 2001"... that will help to... I'm leaving mine with Hez before tonight is over.

On to victory!

Hezekiah Brown runs for Mayor of Hempstead, N.Y.

FROM THE BEGINNING...

Hezekiah Brown (1960-1970)

I was born and raised in a poverty-stricken neighborhood Prichard, Alabama where everyone was poor. There were 11 siblings in my family six boys and five girls. As fate would strike, my mother and father separated, and my father disappeared for 25 years without any contact with the family. It was a tremendous struggle and shock to the family. We became what society labeled as a "broken family". However, instead of a broken family, we became stronger and truly supported the endeavors of each other. We believe that his absence kind of set the stage for our success because early in life we learned that we had to be supportive of each other. Our mother did as much as she could, but she had difficulties because she married early and did not have the skills to get a good paying job. It must be noted that we struggled but never accepted welfare or collected from social services. We were too proud to accept anything from the government. Very quickly, it became apparent that Prichard, Alabama was not the place we wanted to continue to live.

Incidentally, it was viewed by many that the only way out of poverty-stricken Alabama for Africa American males was the military. In fact, very few young people in our neighborhood talked about going to college because during this period, there were not any student loans, grants, or any funds for going to college. Therefore, the only option was going into the military. At this stage of my life, I had dropped out of high school and needed to help support my family. However, my goal was to leave Alabama by any means necessary. This led me to leave Alabama as a migrant farm worker and travel to Virginia where we worked in the field all day as sharecroppers. I was determined to move on and never return to Prichard. Prior to the end of the season, I was able to connect with another group of migrant workers and traveled to New York and subsequently traveled to Florida and returning to New York with this group.

When I returned to New York, I was living in a migrant farm worker's camp on the 2nd floor of a barn. This location was approximately 75 miles from Buffalo, New York. After a relatively short period of time, I contacted my sister, Theresa, and asked her to visit me. Upon her arrival, she observed the barn I was living in and the conditions was so bad until she just started to cry. She informed me that she was coming back the next week and take me to Buffalo, New York. She insisted that I gather all my belongings and be ready to leave at a specific time. When she returned the next week, I walked downstairs with two full grocery bags. My sister was appalled that I could get everything I owned in two grocery bags. In any event, I arrived in Buffalo, New York at the ripe age of 17, uneducated, unemployed, and broke. My sister took me in and started to assist me in finding employment at the Veteran's Hospital in the dietary department. My salary was less than $100.00 every two weeks. I worked at the hospital for approximately three months and later landed a job at a General Motors foundry where I listed my age as 21 and only weighing 145 pounds where the weight requirement was 160 pounds. The key factor here was my salary doubled. My first paycheck at the foundry for 40 hours was $98.60. I remained at the foundry for approximately three months until I turned 18 years old.

ARMY LIFE AND LEARNING

I enlisted into the United States Army on the day I turned 18 on June 21, 1956. Things moved quickly because on July 3, 1956, I was in the Army and arrived at Fort Dix, New Jersey as a private ready to serve my country. Joining the military was the fulfillment of a lifetime dream because it offered discipline, structure, promotional opportunities, leadership skill and organization. My goal was to stay in the Army a minimum of 20 years.

As life presents itself, my life completely changed one day when a group of African American soldiers were on the base and drinking 3.2 beer. A white soldier appeared completely dressed in spit shined boots, tailored uniform with an insignia on the left side of his chest; in our world he was sharp! However, none of us had seen an insignia of such. We questioned him and wanted to know what that insignia was. He told us that the insignia was called "wings". He further explained that to get wings, one must attend rigorous physical training, be mentally tough and complete five qualifying jumps out of an aircraft. He further stressed that there were few African Americans in the Airborne because they were afraid to jump from an aircraft. This remark stunned all of us and we could see that this was leading to a challenge. Here is a white soldier telling a group of African Americans that white men were doing something that African American young men were afraid to do.

After that individual left, we looked at each other in disbelief and felt the challenge. We felt that the entire African American manhood had been attacked by the statement that African American young men were afraid to jump from an airplane!

The moral of this story had a happy ending. The next day all of us signed up for the Airborne and neither of us had ever been on an airplane. In addition, we signed a blood pact, that we would complete the pre-jump school and the airborne training and get our (wings) Parachutist Badge.

Regardless, nothing was going to stop us from finishing this training because, we all were proud brothers and anything the white man could do we could do it better.

The training consisted of three weeks of pre-jump school which included vigorous physical training schedule twice a day. We were not permitted to walk; we had to run everywhere, some instances with full equipment including back packs. Everyone completed the pre-jump school training and went on to jump school. One of the requirements of completing jump school was that every individual had to make at least five acceptable jumps from a 34-foot tower including making five jumps from a moving aircraft. However, I encountered an exceedingly difficult situation the first time I entered the 34-foot tower. I was approached by a sergeant who grabbed me by the collar and used the n.... word and asked me if I was afraid to jump. I quickly responded "No" and at that point he literally kicks me in the rear and out of the tower. I was angry that he had use the N word and was equally as angry that he had used one of the most disrespectful tactics known to mankind and kicked me for no rational reason other than to make me quit.

He was almost successful because my plans were to find a brick or some other weapon and return to the tower to respond to what he had done in a violent way. However, I quickly learned what true friendship and blood packs meant. Chuck — Burley who was one of the soldiers who signed the pact saw me in tears with blood coming from my hand. He asked me what happened. I explained to him what had just happened and gave him my plan to retaliate against this sergeant. He said, "M....F..." put that s...on and go back in the tower. You cannot quit. We must take whatever they throw at us to prove that African Americans are not afraid to jump from an airplane. I sucked it up and went back to the 34-foot tower and ultimately completed five jumps and made five qualifying jumps from an airplane which qualified me to receive the parachutist badge and my WINGS.

There was a huge ceremony for those who had completed jump school and the group commander actually pinned the wings on each soldier. I must admit that it was one of the proudest moments of my young life. While completing the training was an extremely difficult task, it was worth it. In fact, after completing jump school, it gave me self-confidence and I learned that an individual can do anything they want if they set goals, and let nothing stop you from attaining the goal you set for yourself.

During my tenure in the Armed Forces, I learned how to work with people and found it to be educationally rewarding. It taught me the importance of teamwork brought to the surface some of my leadership qualities, thus, instilling in me a sense of pride and self-esteem. One of the positive things that contributed to my self- discipline, was being appointed Acting Sergeant as a Private. That appointment helped to build my self-confidence, which I desperately needed. It became apparent to me, that in order to be a good leader, one must set examples for those under your supervision. The leadership role was new to me at the age of eighteen. I accepted it as a challenge and become a model Soldier.

I remained in the Army for two years, and served for four years in the US Reserve. Upon release, I received an Honorable Discharge and was awarded the Good Conduct Medal.

LITTLE ROCK ARKANSAS 62 YEARS LATER

Hezekiah Brown with 6 of the Little Rock Nine

As I reminisce about my Little Rock, Arkansas experience 62 year ago as a member of the 101st Airborne, 327 Airborne Battle Group, United States Army, it brings back bitter-sweet memories. In 1957, September 4th and 25th are significant and historic days in our American History. September 4, 1957 was the first day of forced school integration at Central High School in Little Rock, Arkansas and September 25th 1957 was the first day Federal Troops was ordered into Little Rock Arkansas by President Dwight D. Eisenhower to protect the Little Rock Nine as they attempted to integrate the High school, Thelma Mothershed Wair, Minnijean Brown Tricky, Jefferson Thomas, Terrence Roberts, Carlotta Walls Lanier, Gloria Ray Karlmark, Ernest Green, Elizabeth Eckford, and Melba Pattillo Beal.

I can recall the day we arrived, as soldiers, we had mixed emotions and was pleasantly surprised at the actions taken by the President, and the resident of Little Rock were equally as surprised with the unprecedented action of President Eisenhower.

As we were transported by trucks from the airport, we could see and hear the mobs standing along the roadway shouting racial epithets with weapons, baseball bats and ax handles and one could feel the anger. This was the day after the Governor of Arkansas had removed the National Guard from the school where they were there to prevent the Little Rock Nine from integrating the school. (By removing the National Guard from the school, the students were exposed to the angry crowds without protection). Therefore President Dwight D. Eisenhower ordered Federal Troops into Little Rock Central High School to protect the African American Students (Little Rock Nine) attending school by orders of the Supreme Court Brown vs the Board of Education decision.

Upon arrival, in Little Rock with our integrated armed forces, the decision had been made by the hierarchy of the Army that African American soldiers would not be part of the soldiers protecting and escorting the students because it would add fuel to the fire. I along with all of the African American soldiers were extremely disappointed and angered by the action of the Army hierarchy in preventing African American soldiers from participating in what we termed was more of our fight than the white soldiers.

However, in retrospect, it was the right decision that the African American soldiers did not participate in the activities at the school because the focus would have been taken away from the goal of protecting the student and the school probably never would have been integrated.

The Brown vs the Board of Education decision was not accepted by the white community, the Governor and some politicians. In fact, 100 Senators and Congressmen was also opposed to the decision and stated that this decision would never be implemented. There were many who fought hard to reverse the decision to integrate the schools because by integrating the schools it would permeate into other areas. In fact the Brown vs the board of Education decision was rendered in 1954 and faced tremendous opposition predominately from southern whites. It took 3 years to move toward school integration which still faced opposition. Governor Orval Faubus became internationally known during the Little Rock Crisis of 1957, when he used the Arkansas National Guard to stop Africans Americans from attending Little Rock Central High School.

The ironic part about the issue of school integration in Arkansas is that only one of the Little Rock Nine actually graduated from Central High School during this period of turmoil. Ernest Green became the first and only one of the Little Rock Nine to graduate from Central High School in a ceremony attended by Dr. Martin Luther King Jr.

During the next school year, the voters chose to shut down all of the High Schools in Little rock rather than integrate them. So, all of the other students graduated from other high schools or via correspondence classes or other States.

50 years later

In September of 2007 my wife and I attended the 50th anniversary of the Little Rock Nine. At the 50th anniversary the atmosphere was quite different. African American students attended Central High School without Solider escorts. It was a great celebration where black and whites came together in a sincere fashion to celebrate the making of history. The ceremony was attended by former President Bill Clinton, Hillary Clinton, Congressman John Lewis was the (Keynote speaker); Senators, Congressmen, Local Elected Officials Former Democratic and Republican Officials, Civil Right Leaders, Dignitaries, all celebrated this historic event joyfully. The Mayor who was white kept his children out of school to attend the festivities.

In essence out of all bad come some good; out of all good come some bad.

Hezekiah Brown

THE JOURNEY BEGINS

After the Army, I returned to the Tonawanda Metal Casting Plant, but I was not the same person. I wanted to further exploit my leadership abilities. I started to get involved in any and all union activities. I volunteered to serve on any standing committee within the Local and was elected Chairman of the education committee. As Chairman of this committee, I was designated by the President to attend classes on learning teaching techniques and teaching the teacher. After completing the course, I was able to share with my co-workers what I had learned and was instrumental in getting them involved.

During a thirteen-week strike, I taught every day. Instead of having all of the members walk the picket line, half had to perform picket duties, while the others were scheduled into the classrooms to learn why they were on strike.

We saw this as a golden opportunity to teach the members the history of the Labor Movement, current issues in contract negotiations, importance of the grievance procedure, and Labor History. The teaching endeavor was successful and served two purposes for me personally. It gave me an opportunity to meet each member, and the members saw me contributing to a time of crisis. It was also a great opportunity for me to become confident and effective as a teacher.

Shortly after the strike, a number of my co-workers encouraged me in run for the position of Alternate Committeeman. I served in that position for four years. During that same period, I was elected to the Executive Board, and became Chairman of the Trustees. The duties of the Trustees, according to the By-laws, were to perform bi-annual audits, attend all Executive Board meetings, in addition to reviewing all requests all requests for payment by the members.

Upon assuming this role, I had no experience in bookkeeping. I enrolled in a course in bookkeeping and completed the course in preparation for this assignment. The next general election, I ran for District Committeeman and won by a landslide. Subsequently, I ran for the Local Bargaining Committee and won that election, also.

This led me to my first experience of being involved with contract negotiations. It was an experience I will never forget.

IT IS ALL ABOUT NEGOTIATION

There was another long strike. Originally, I was of the opinion that the Union was supposed to submit proposals and wait until the employer met their demands. I had no idea that the employer would question the Union about their proposals, and the Union was obligated to justify each and every proposal. I did not understand the interaction between the chief negotiators. As negotiations continued, I learned the do's and don'ts of collective bargaining. That is what I now refer to as my "crash course" in collective bargaining. I learned the political as well as the individual approach including the departmental aspect of collective bargaining. I learned that one must have trust and respect for everyone serving on a bargaining team. In addition, one must understand the role and interest of all involved. I further learned that collective bargaining is based on issues, not emotion, and must be treated as such.

Part of our Local bargaining entailed resolving all grievances in concert with resolving the contract. I was appointed Chairman of that committee. Here, I learned the art of grievance negotiations and the timeliness and importance of compromise. During these negotiations, I was involved in resolving more that 300 grievances, including a number of discharges.

That led me to my next endeavor. After gaining the respect and trust of my co-workers, I was elected President of my Local. The Local consisted of 3,500 skilled and non-skilled workers. I was the youngest person to ever be elected to that position. Serving in the role as President, I was able to learn the administrative side along with expanding my knowledge of the collective bargaining side. Along with my duties as President, came other opportunities and responsibilities. I was the chief spokesperson for approximately 150 cafeteria workers who were not a part of the General Motors – UAW structure. My duties were to handle grievances at the Stop II level and present cases at the arbitration level. In addition, it was my responsibility to negotiate their contract separately from the General Motors – UAW contracts.

Other duties carried me to the international level by being appointed to the International Resolution Committee and serving on the Steering

Committee which elected Leonard Woodcock to his first term as President of the UAW. Incidently, Leonard Woodcock became the Ambassador to Russia under President Jimmy Carter. I was also elected Vice-President of the International Foundry Wage and Hour Conference and elected as an alternate top negotiator for all foundry workers in the United States and Canada. I was appointed Chairperson of the New York State Fair Employment Practice Committee. I was further involved in the community by serving on the Western New York Political Action Committee and was involved in voter registration year-round. Under my administration, our Local was the first in Western New York to have in-plant voter registration. I negotiated the first on-premise joint alcoholic rehabilitation program in my area.

Over-all, my experience as a labor leader was a great experience. I often refer to that experience as my period of education. What I learned as a practitioner cannot be learned in a classroom. My negotiating skills were sharpened on a day to day basis, my community involvement was grossly expanded and most of all, I was afforded the opportunity to learn while doing.

GENERAL MOTORS AND UNITED AUTO WORKERS UNION EXPERIENCE

My career in Labor relations started in 1962 while I was employed by General Motors Corporation at the Tonawanda Metal Casting Plant. The name Metal Casting Plant was a fancy name for foundry. There were a variety of different departments, skilled trades, supervision, inspection were all white. Other departments such as the cleaning and core room and the foundry were predominately African Americans who had migrated from southern states to work in the automobile factories. Many of those employees hired were by and large uneducated and previously worked on farms as sharecroppers. While the plant itself was integrated in hiring, it still was defacto segregated through departments. While a majority of the employees were African American, they were relegated to the unskilled jobs regardless of their educational background. The skilled trades which consisted of electricians, millwrights and machinist were all white including supervision and the inspection department. In fact, the plant was openly segregated by classifications and departments. However, the segregation was not an issue with the vast majority of the employees because a high number was from the segregated south. They were probably earning three times as much as they had earned on the farms and menial jobs in the deep segregated South and hard work, excessive heat and heavy lifting was not an issue.

I worked in the cleaning room where engine parts were cleaned through chipping, sand blasting and grinded prior to being shipped to the assembly plants.

The work in the foundry was exceedingly difficult, laborious, extremely hot and required an inordinate amount of lifting and working in excessive heat. In fact, one of the predominate requirements to being employed in the foundry was the size of the individual. Individuals had to pass a rigid physical examination and must weigh the minimum of 160 pounds. Individuals were required to wear safety glasses, shoes, ear plugs and respirators to protect themselves from the dangerous surrounding environment.

The plant was like a ghetto or plantation within a city where all the ill of poor and uneducated African Americans took place. There were individuals who were addicted to alcohol, hard drugs, loan sharks who charged individuals weekly fees of 25% to 50% to borrow money. There were crap games which started on Thursday nights in the locker rooms and continued through Saturday. Individuals could openly play illegal numbers through department number writes. In fact, one could play numbers on credit. One could purchase drugs, stolen goods and in some instances, prostitutes were smuggled into the plant to do business.

In addition, individuals in some departments were treated like they were still on the plantation while some departments treated their employees with respect. Of course, we had a local union that was strong and was extremely capable of handling disputes between management and the employees. However, the working conditions were horrible due to the antiquated and outdated machinery. In some area's individuals were forced to handle extremely hot parts with their hands with inadequate protective gloves and others poured hot liquid iron into moldings which was extremely dangerous and unsafe.

After observing the many injustices perpetrated on my co-workers, I decided to challenge the unjust and discriminatory system. Incidentally, I was the youngest employee employed because I had advanced my age by 4 years to qualify for the job. When I started work at the plant, I was only 17 years old. When making written application for the job, I stated on the application that I was 21 years old so they would not ask for age verification.

I challenged the most bigoted, and inhumane supervisor in the plant. His name was Walter Weiss. He was mean and treated the employees who worked under his jurisdiction like they were still on the plantation. After I started to challenge him, my co-workers became concerned for me and they thought that he would fire me. However, I survived his verbal assaults and threats and my co-worker encouraged me to run for a union position because they had observed me being able to survive and out maneuver this supervisor. I ran for alternate Committeeman and was reelected and subsequently ran for the District Committeeman and was elected to the plant wide collective bargaining committee. The plant wide collective bargaining team members were full time positions. I subsequently was elected president and at 32 years old was the youngest person elected president of this local of approximately 3,500 members.

Since our local was the only local within three states: New York, New Jersey, and Pennsylvania, that could elect an African American president, it provided me with many local, state, and national opportunities. My first appointment was chairman of the New York State Fair Employment Practice Committee (FEPC) and elected as a delegate to the UAW International Convention and appointed to the constitutional committee. The constitutional committee was the committee that reviewed the resolutions submitted to the National Bargaining committee by various locals throughout the United States and Canada. I had the honor and opportunity to present resolutions to over 5000 Union Delegates. Ted Kennedy was one of the keynote speakers at the convention.

During the Foundry wage and hour conference, I met an individual who was President of a UAW Local in Detroit, Michigan. His name was Lawrence (Larry) Berry. We became the best of friends and he was the individual who initially approached me regarding employment with the Federal Mediation and Conciliation Service. Larry had been appointed a Commissioner with the Federal Mediation & Conciliation for three months and made some quick observations. His observations revealed that the Agency employed over 240 Field Mediators and there were few African American. He informed me that the White House had made the same observations. In fact, it was noted that President Nixon was running for re-election and wanted to hire more minorities in mid-level position to try and influence/persuade African Americans to vote for him. I was stunned because my local never used a Mediator in the negotiations. In fact, I did not have a clue of what the role of a Mediator was in collective bargaining. However, with his encouragement, I said yes, I would apply for the job to satisfy him frankly knowingly that I would not be accepted because of my lack of knowledge regarding mediation.

Incidentally, in order to become a Mediator, individuals were required to have a minimum of 7 years' experience in collective bargaining including a clean record and never being a part of any subversive or anti-government groups. With the continuous urging of Larry Barry, I submitted my application and with the assistance of Leonard Woodcock, International President of the United Auto Workers and Vice President Nelson "Jack" Edwards, I was selected to serve as a Commissioner with the Federal Mediation and Conciliation Service.

Now here is the catch 22, I knew I did not have the full credentials to become a Federal Mediator. However, because of my basic philosophy that I learned while in the military, I honestly believed that I could learn to do anything anyone else could do. Then the light in my head went off! I was totally unaware of the magnitude of my discovery regarding my research which ultimately lead to Foundry and Forge workers receiving 25 years and out retirement with full benefits.

I recalled that I was on the resolution committee for the Foundry Wage and Hour Committee. Due to the horrible conditions we worked under, we were fighting extremely hard for a resolution to be submitted to the National Bargaining Team requesting that the committee negotiate a "25 years and out" for Foundry and Forge workers. Every instance when we raised the issue, we were informed that There was no hard evidence or research that foundry and forge workers became ill or had more deadly ailments than other General Motors employees.

In the early 1970's, after returning from the Foundry Wage Conference, I call my secretary into my office and asked her how many retirees were still alive? She informed me that it was approximately 100 retired employees that we were still in contact with. We developed a questionnaire that had the following questions: How long did you work at the foundry? Do you have any of the following ills: Heart problems, respiratory illness, hearing, breathing, high blood pressure, etc.? We sent the questionnaire out to the retirees and requested that they make a check on the questionnaire if they had either 1, 2, 3, 4 or any other illness. The questionnaires came back with 98% of those retirees adversely affected and some had silicosis or all the above ailments. I reviewed the information and compiled it not knowing what I was going to do with it.

I attended the next Foundry Wage and Hour Conference and took this report with me. After being properly recognized by the Chairman, I stated to the Chairman and other conference members that with all of the knowledge and education, I was appalled that the Union and General Motors Representative could not do the research to grant Foundry and Forge Workers 25 years and out. I remember when I started to explain what my research had shown the secretary cut the power from the recording machine. I stopped talking and insisted that the recorder be turned back on. With support and applause from the conference members it was turned back on and my report became a part of the official record.

After returning home to Buffalo, New York, a few days later, I received a telephone call from International Representative C. O. Kelly. He informed me that the International President, Leonard Woodcock wanted to talk to me and that I should come to Detroit, Michigan. I became a bit apprehensive and was a little intimidated that the President wanted to talk to me!

In a relative short period of time, I travelled to Detroit and was met at the door by C. O. Kelly. He asked me where the report was. I explained to him that he had not requested that I bring a report of my research/finding. However, we proceeded to a large room where President Woodcock, Vice President Irving Bluestone, and the Secretary Treasurer were present. I was really intimidated in the presence of the top three officers of this powerful Union with a membership in excessive of one million bargaining unit employees. President Woodcock was very cordial and friendly and welcomed me into his office. We had a brief conversation regarding the research I had reported at the foundry Wage and Hour conference. He asked me about the research that I had done and asked me for a copy. I explained to him that I did not bring a copy of the research with me. I informed him that I would send him a copy upon my return to Buffalo. Upon my return to Buffalo, New York, I sent a copy of my research to C. O. Kelly who passed it on to the President.

In actuality, I really did not know the magnitude of what I had discovered and did not give it any further thought until a few years later. I learned that General Motors and the UAW had negotiated a "25 years and out" for foundry and forge Workers at the next contract…I do not have any hard evidence that my innocent research contributed to General Motors and the UAW negotiating the 25 years and out for foundry and forge Worker. However, I am convinced that my research sparked the researches and provided an avenue for them to perform the research that ultimately led to the 25 years and out retirement plan for Foundry and Forge workers after I was selected to become a Federal Mediator.

I further believe that the reason it was so easy for me to become one of the youngest Federal Mediators in the history of the Agency was due to my discovery. I did something that all the General Motors and UAW research Official claimed that they could not do. My research showed that 98% of those employees retired had some form or all the ills pointed out in my research. Therefore, rather than give me credit for developing this research, it was to their advantage to get me out of the GM-UAW circle so I would not receive credit for my revelation.

In conclusion, I do not believe that I would have been selected as a Federal Mediator if I had not innocently discovered a method to reveal the ills of Foundry and Forge Workers.

Class Picture

SELECTED AS A FEDERAL MEDIATOR

On October 23, 1972, I was hired as a Commissioner with the Federal Mediation and Conciliation Service; I was ecstatic, excited, and frightened at the same time because I was unfamiliar with the role of a federal mediator. However, my ego showed up and I realized that if any other individual could mediate, I could too.

I spent two weeks in Washington, DC and returned to Buffalo, New York. Upon my return to Buffalo, I was initially assigned to the Buffalo Office with three other Mediators, Commissioner's Sam Sackman, Joseph Bania and George O'Keefe. I was only assigned to Buffalo, New York office for two months. While I was assigned to the Buffalo Office, I was exposed to three of the Agency's top mediators. One of the things that stands out In my career was the different styles of mediators. I believe I learned the most from Sam Sackman.

Sam freely gave me mediation tips and offered me tremendous survival skills. He said that I would have to watch my back because of the blatant racism of some of the mediators. He also gave me probably the best advice one could give. He informed me that in my career as a mediator, my colleagues would be critical of me if I did not do enough work and others would also be critical if you worked too hard. He stated those being critical; let them criticize you for working too hard rather than not carrying your load. That was great advice that stuck with me forever.

In January of 1973, I was assigned to the New York office of the Federal Mediation & Conciliation Service.

Upon my arrival, I was introduced to the Regional Director, Frank Brown. I believe Frank was in his 70's and still going strong. I was eager to learn how to mediate Labor-Management disputes but hit a wall. Learning how to mediate was an "on the job" training process. Trainees would have to accompany other veteran mediators to learn the skill of mediation. However, I hit a wall because most of the veteran mediators would not permit me to go on assignments with them. It was a kind of suddle racism that Sam Sackman had warned me about. I was relegated to reading books and sitting in the office for approximately six months and was extremely disappointed. There was one other African American veteran mediator in the New York Office who had over forty years of Government Service. I thought he would help me or serve as my mentor. To no avail, he ignored me too!

Then one morning, this elderly Mediator Matt Miller came into my office and asked me what was wrong. I explained to him my dilemma and lack of opportunities to be trained as a mediator. He said, *"I am going to fix that"*. In fact, he went on to say, *I am going to make you the best mediator on this Universe"*. That is when my "on-the-job" training started.

Matt was truly God sent because I was able to travel with him and begin to learn mediation skills and got to know the parties involved in various disputes. After other mediators observed the interest Matt had taken in me, they started to warm up to me and offered assistance. Thereafter, I began to receive my own case load which was fantastic! Initially, I received assignment of small bargaining units and graduated to larger case assignment.

I was involved in numerous high visible disputes within the New York City area. The most notable was United Parcel and IBT Local 804. This strike lasted thirteen weeks and UPS came awfully close to shutting down its New York City operation. It by far was one of the most difficult strikes in the North East due to the economic impact on small business. There were a large number of small businesses in New York City who did not have storage space and relied on the next day delivery of UPS. During the extended strike, many small businesses went out of business due to the strike.

One of the issues that kept the strike going so long the fact that one of the Union Business Agents was killed by a UPS truck the first night of the strike. He was the President of IBT Local 804 best friend. Of course, this added another dimension to the strike…it became an emotional and economic dispute. In fact, there was such a dislike between the parties that it was exceedingly difficult to get them to meet face to face. In fact, the negotiations were subsequently move to Washington D.C where William Usury, the National Director and Special Assistant to President Gerald Ford entered the dispute. After days and long sessions neither side's position changed. Therefore, Director Usury assigned to the National Representative John Zaccanarro and me to take as much time as needed and write a recommendation so close that the parties could not refuse to accept our recommendation. It took John and me three days to complete writing the recommendations, in fact, when we completed writing the recommendations, and presented it to the Director, it was approximately 3:00 a.m. in the thirteen weeks of the strike. The Director knew the importance of getting this dispute resolved because the two U. S. Senators, Congressmen, Local Elected officials including the Mayor of New York City, Abraham Beam knew the impact of the threat to close down this operation and the devastating impact it was having on local business and the jobs involved.

Director Usury stated that we had to do something non-traditional to end this dispute. He said that we were going to submit the recommendations to the parties in separate caucuses and inform them that the written recommendations would be submitted to *The Washington Post* and *The New York Times* the following morning. This action truly got both parties attention because we captured 95% of all the important issues in our recommendations. Both parties initially question the authority and the legal implications if this recommendation was released to the newspaper without authorization of the parties of interest. However, this bold action taken by the Director out maneuvered the parties and forced them to the first face to face meeting in seven weeks. During several meetings, the parties utilized the written recommendation as a road map to negotiate a final agreement that was ratified by the members within 24 hours which ended the strike. Again, I did not personally recognize the magnitude or the far-reaching implications of my contributions to saving thousands of jobs and businesses in New York City. In fact, Mayor Abe Beam invited us to City Hall and personally thanks us for our contributions to assisting in ending the strike.

Another significant and important dispute I was involved in was the seven-week strike between The League of Voluntary Hospitals and 1199 Health and Hospital Workers Union that involved approximately 100,000 workers.

Hezekiah Brown with Basil Patterson,
Lt. Governor David Patterson, 1st lady Hillary Clinton

This dispute was even more significant because during this dispute I had the opportunity to work with one of the most competent and well-respected individuals in the Labor-Management profession, my mentor, Basil Patterson. In addition, I had the opportunity to meet the Commissioner of Labor for the State of New York, Tom Harnett. The three of us had the task of mediating the dispute between the parties. We spent many days and night and long hours trying to find the key to end the strike. I recall Basil and Tim asked me if I would ever consider working for the State of New York. I informed them that leaving the Federal Mediation & Conciliation Service had not crossed my mind because it was the best job in the world! I went on to say that the only job for the State of New York that would interest me was the Chairman of the New York State Mediation Board which was a position appointed by the Governor. Deep down inside, again, I felt that this position was well beyond my reach. We were instrumental in resolving the strike including developing a great personal relationship.

In addition, I was subsequently selected as an Arbitrator to hear and render a decision that actually revolutionized the Health Care Industry regarding "Every Other Weekend Off". The decision was issued in 1989. The award read as follows:

"The Arbitrator, noting that unscheduled absences from work on a scheduled weekend workday interferes with the operation of the Hospital and imposes serious inconvenience on other employees who come to work as scheduled, determines and directs as follows:

1. *Employees who were on the payroll of the Hospital prior to October 12, 1986, and have continued on the payroll thereafter, and were on an every other weekend work schedule and not previously required to make up unscheduled absences as of October 12, 1986 will not be required to make up unscheduled absences as of October 12, 1986 will not be required to make up (a) the first three (3) days of absence on scheduled weekend work days due to illness or injury absent unjustified use of sick leave or (b) Absence on scheduled weekend work days due to vacation, holidays and paid or unpaid leaves (including but not limited to leave for which disability or worker compensation is received).*

2. *Employees who were on the payroll of the Hospital prior to October 12, 1986 and have continued on the payroll thereafter, and were on an every other weekend schedule and previously required to make up unscheduled absences on a scheduled weekend work day due to sick leave (including paid and unpaid sick days). Only; they will not be required to make up absences on scheduled weekend workdays due to vacations, holidays and paid or unpaid leaves (including but not limited to leave for which disability or workers compensation is received).*

3. *Employees who are hired on or after October 12, 1986 and have been or are on an every other weekend work schedule may be required to make up unscheduled absences on a scheduled weekend work days due to sick leave (including pair of unpaid sick days) only; they will not be required to make up absences on scheduled weekend work days due to vacation, holidays and paid or unpaid leaves including but not limited to leave for which disability or workers compensation is received)."*

The above award set the tone and offered the basics for The League of Voluntary Hospitals and District 119 of the Health and Hospital Workers Union to negotiate a universal agreement covering the issue of "Every

Other Weekend Off" for Hospital Workers with some minor exceptions. That agreement ultimately permeated throughout the health care industry nationwide. This landmark decision positively affected millions of health care workers. Again, this was another instance where my involvement and decision impacted millions of workers and I did not at the time recognize the importance or the magnitude of the decision.

I also received mediation assignment in the U. S. Virgin Island and Puerto Rico. I was assigned to mediate a dispute between the Virgin Island government and the Virgin Island Nurses Association. In addition, I mediated the dispute between the Ademco Alarm Company and RWDSU, District 65 in Puerto Rico. Additionally, I was instrumental in assisting the establishment of the first joint area wide Labor-Management Committee in the Virgin Island which had far reaching implications regarding labor peace in the Virgin Islands.

Along this journey, Regional Director Paul Yeager acknowledged my exceptional commitment to the Federal Mediation and Conciliation Service by mediating more than 200 assignments per year. In fact, he nominated me to the President of the United States to receive the Presidential Community Service Award. I received the Presidential Community Service Award from President Ronal Reagan for my work in the community. In addition, I received numerous recognitions from the FMCS for outstanding performance and high-quality awards.

W. J. Usery, Jr., Director   2-3-75

ATTENTION; Norman Walker-
Chairman authority Committee

Paul Yager, Director, Region I

    Recommendation for High Quality Performance Pay Increase.
    Commissioner Hezekiah Brown

Commissioner Hezekiah Brown performs at a consistently high level
of effectiveness in all tasks. In addition, he is a valuable member
of our Regional Office Community. He is helpful in the training of
new mediators; he is concerned about the effective operation of the
office; he cooperates in every possible way with the Regional
Director, Assistant Regional Director and Regional Coordinator.

Commissioner Brown is taking courses to improve his own skills.
He is always available for assignment at odd hours and on normally
non-work days. Commissioner Brown has performed his mediation'
assignments in a highly effective manner. He is able to establish
acceptability in situations where the FMCS has previously encountered difficulty. As an example, he was able to participate in the
recent Teamsters-UPS negotiation, in the face of the parties' prior
avoidance of mediation in all previous negotiations. The UPS assignment in many ways is a fine example of Commissioner Brown's outstanding pefformance. In addition to establishing his acceptability in
the face of previous coolness toward FMCS by the parties', he was
able to maintain constructive collective bargaining in spite of a
prolonged strike over very strongly held positions by the parties.
In fact, as the strike grew older, Commissioner Brown's relations
with the parties strengthened because they realized that when the
time came for a settlement , he would be the chief factor in achieving it.

The settlement was, achieved by bringing the parties to the N. O. for
the final sessions. It was Commissioner Brown's sense of timing and
his knowledge of the issues which provided the basis for the N. O.
activity which culminated in the settlement.

Commissioner Brown has also opened the door for the FMCS in other
Teamster negotiations, such as the Emery Air Freight dispute at
Kennedy Airport where a very delicate situation was handled with
great skill. The Newspaper Guild, Distributive Workers, Retail
clerks and IAM are enthusiastic fans of Commissioner Brown. Notably,

large groups of sophisticated New York management attorneys seek
his assistance in a variety of cases. Many of them first sought
his assistance in situations where race might be a factor but now
they no longer consider that. Many of them have indicated to me
that they prefer Commissioner Brown in all their negotiations.

Commissioner Brown performs Technical Assistance assignments effectively and enthusiastically. He is engaged in such an assignment
as a part of the UPS settlement. He also participated in the recent highly successful Relationship by Objectives Program at the
Georgia Pacific Co. in Maine.

Commissioner Brown is a walking Public Relations spokesman for the
FMCS. He participates in many community activities such as Career
Day functions at local schools. He uses his mediation skills in
his own neighborhood as a member of a community team for resolving
disputes. He attends IRRA meetings and he has participated in
formal PR programs such as one we did for the Federal Executive
Board of Northern New Jersey.

I am particularly pleased with Commissioner Brown's conscientious-
ness in reporting. He reports promptly, completely and he knows
how to report all the relevant and material information without
rambling.

Commissioner Brown is a prime example of the enthusiastic and competent young mediators we should be encouraging. I am convinced
that he will continue to perform at this high level throughout his
career. Therefore, I urge prompt favorable attention to this
recommendation.

FY/ls

THE NEW YORK TIMES
FEDERAL MEDIATOR TAKES CORNELL POST

BY THE ASSOCIATED PRESS
DECEMBER 26, 1984

Hezekiah Brown, a one-time high school dropout and factory worker who became one of the Federal Government's top labor mediators, is resigning to become the head of a department at Cornell University.

During his 12 years with the Federal Mediation and Conciliation Service, Brown has handled some of the region's touchiest dispute, including the six weeklong hospital strike this summer and the nine week-long Con-Edison walkouts in 1983.

His resignation take effect, January 3, when the 46 years old mediator become the Director of Labor-Management programs at Cornell University Extension in New York City.

"Hez is going to be missed very much, because, not only has he been an effective mediator, but a fine colleague," said the Regional Director, Paul Yeager. "He has spanned a tremendous range of accomplishments and broken racial barriers. He is an inspiration, and I don't think that's too strong a word."

A native of Prichard, Alabama, Brown moved to Buffalo, New York at the age of 16 and dropped out of high school. He applied for work at a local General Motors Metal Casting plant, inflating his age by five years and his weight by 15 pounds and got a job as a grinder.

In his 20's, Brown became active in the United Auto Workers and in 1970, was elected President of UAW, Local 1173, the same year, He passed his high school diploma equivalency test.

Two years later, Brown resigned from the union to join the U. S. Government as one of the youngest labor mediators, and one of the few blacks. Soon, he was receiving major assignments in the city, Long Island, Westchester, County, Connecticut, Puerto Rico, and the Virgin Islands.

In 1974, he gained national prominence as the peacemaker in the 13-week Teamster strike against United Parcel Service.

Afterward Brown took management and workers to a secluded place for a three-day seminar to talk about day-to-day problems. Then he helped them write a Relation by Objective Program which both sides signed. "Before we started the program, UPS suffered 10 to 12 wildcat strikes a year during the life of the contract, "Brown said recently. "Since the implementation of the RBO program, believe that they experienced only on wildcat strike in 10 years."

Brown proved especially effective with university professors, and handled disputes at Long Island University, Adelphi University, Bridgeport University, Wagner College, Columbia University and Barnard College.

At the same time, he was pursuing his own education, and in 1983, he graduated with a Bachelor of Science degree from Empire State College, a division of State University of New York.

Last year, President Regan awarded the Presidential Award for Community Service to Mr. Brown, who also was a recipient of the Black Achiever in Industry Award. He also sits on Advisory boards to Pan American Airways, Work in America Institute, New York Institute of Technology, Hempstead High School Vocational Education Committee and serves on the Hempstead for Hofstra Scholarship Committee.

By 1984, I had reached the level of an accomplish mediator and was involved in numerous high visible mediations, such as College and Universities, The University of Bridgeport, Adelphi University, Long Island University, Southampton University Brooklyn College Health Care institutions, newspapers: *The New York Times, The new York Daily News, New York Post, The Amsterdam News, National Black Network News, Health Care Industry, etc.* In addition, I had the distinct honor to work with the legendary mediator Ted Kheel. In fact, I was given credit for mediating the dispute that actually saved the *New York Post* when it was struggling financially. I made the recommendation as an alternative to laying off employees that the bargaining unit employees go on a four-day work week schedule. That proposal was accepted, and the threat of a strike disappeared, and the newspaper continues to survive as of today.

In my opinion and the opinion of others, I had mastered the mediation field and was lacking full knowledge in one area, teaching. One of the requirements of being a complete mediator, individual had to become proficient in a component in establishing joint-Labor-Management Committees and providing technical service to the parties. Therefore, in order to sharpen and increase my teaching skills, I volunteered at Cornell University Extension to teach for free to increase my teaching skills. I co-taught with Carolyn Wittenberg and Peggy Leibowitz the first semester. The second semester I taught alone and received raving reviews and excellent evaluations from the students. Carolyn Wittenberg was impressed with my teaching and stated to me that if she ever became the Director of the New York City Extension, she would ask me to come to work for Cornell University Extension. Personally, I thought she was just making small talk or attempting to make me feel good. I was subsequently offered to teach as an Adjunct Professor for pay, teaching, Collective Bargaining, Contract Administration and Labor History. I was the happiest guy in the world! I had the best job in the world as a Federal Mediator and now offered to teach at an Ivy League School.

Six months later, Carolyn Wittenberg became the Director of the New York City Extension of Cornell University. By the time she became the Director, I had been assigned to the Hempstead office of the Federal Mediation and Conciliation Service. I was extremely comfortable because my office was located approximately five minutes from my home, and I was deeply engaged in the community. However, she called me and asked me if I was ready to come to work for Cornell University? In fact, this was the second time I was offered a position that I did not think I had the credentials to perform the job. Frankly, I simply did not know what to tell her. I was looking for a way to say no or find some reason without telling her that I did not feel I was qualified for the position. I invited her to my office for further discussion and explained to her that she was asking me to take a position at an Ivy League school and at the time I only had an Associate Degree. She explained to me that individuals did not need an advanced degree to teach at a college or university. They needed individual who had exceptional practical on the job experience with an outstanding track record. After that conversation, I still was not sure that I wanted to leave this highly visible job that offered me and my family job security. I then figured out that I could reject the job based on the salary. She destroyed that approach because she offered me $15,000 more than I expected. I told her that I would consider her offer. I was in a quandary. I wanted to say yes, but I was concerned about my credentials. It dawned on me that I could return to college and get the degrees required for the job. It took me three months to finally accept her offer. She even permitted me to pick my title. In January 1985, I became the Director of Labor-Management programs at Cornell University Extension.

Upon my acceptance of the position, I enrolled at Empire State College and due to my years of experience, I was teaching a course on mediation prior to receiving my bachelor's degree. In fact, I developed the mediation curriculum and taught at Empire State College for my last nine credits. I later taught several courses at Empire State College after I graduated.

While at Cornell University, I became the in-house mediator who intervened in dispute between co-workers, supervisors, and employees, Chief Negotiator for Cornell University Extension, and served as Acting Director, Developed a five day Dispute Resolution Certificate Program that attracted students from as far away as Bangladesh, South America, Italy and other foreign countries. In addition, I was instrumental in developing a joint Labor-Management Program that was in demand from both labor and management that brought in tremendous financial resources to the university. I further taught anger management, conflict resolution, collective bargaining, mediation skills, managing change, contract administration and arbitration.

UNITED STATES GOVERNMENT

memorandum

DATE: December 1, 1980

REPLY TO
ATTN OF: Paul Yager, Director, Region 1

SUBJECT: Recommendation for High Quality Increase - Comm. Hezekiah Brown

TO: Mr. Edward McMahon
    Chairman, Awards Committee

Commissioner Hezekiah Brown entered on duty October 1972. He was promoted to GS-13 October 1973 and to GS-14 December 1975. In December 1980 he reaches the 14/5 level. In July 1977 Comm. Brown was transferred to the Hempstead Field Office. He had been awarded a high quality promotion in February 1975 which was wiped out in December of that year when he was promoted to GS-14.

Comm. Brown is an outstanding mediator. He is capable of handling any and every kind of assignment. He has the ability to gain the confidence of the most sophisticated negotiators in the business. He is one of the most requested mediators in Region I. He deals effectively with university presidents and faculties as well as with teamsters and construction workers. He made notable contributions to the successful negotiations in two major utility cases in New York City, Brooklyn and Union Gas Co. with IBEW and the TWU and the Consolidated Edison Co. with IBEW and the Utility Workers. He recently completed negotiations wih the Brooklyn Campus Faculty of Long Island University with Long Island University. This was one of the most difficult negotiations we have had in recent years because of the complexity of the issues. In spite of the necessity for Commissioner Brown to play the heavy with both the administration and the faculty, they have both gone out of their way to commend his efforts to me. Another difficult negotiation in recent months involved the New York Racing Association and the IBEW Tote Operators. Vince McDonnell represented the employer and made a point of instructing Commissioner Brown as to how to handle this assignment. Nevertheless, Brown was instrumental in helping the parties achieve a settlement. Brown has also been very effective in Health Care assignments and has worked with me on the League of Voluntary Hospitals-1199 negotiations the last several rounds.. Commissioner Brown is an enthusiastic Technical Assistance performer. He has been a leader in handling R80s. We have used him to train Region I mediators as well as mediators from other Regions in the R80 technique. The high regard in which Commissioner Brown is held by be Labor-Management Community is attested to by his recent election to the Chairman of the newly organized IRRA Chapter on Long Island. I heartily recommend a High Quality promotion for Commissioner Brown.

OPTIONAL FORM NO. 10
(REV. 1-80)
GSA FPMR (41 CFR) 101-11.6
5010-114

Commissioner Brown's position description and the performance standards for the position were thoroughly reviewed prior to the submission of this recommendation. I certify that the employee's performance of all the important job elements substantially exceeds normal requirements, that the remainder of the performance exceeds normal requirements, and that such performance in this position shows promise of continuing at this high level in the future.

Paul Yager   December 1, 1980

PY/pm

cc: Evelyn Baker

FEDERAL MEDIATION AND CONCILIATION SERVICE

UNITED STATES GOVERNMENT

26 Federal Plaza, Room 2937
New York, New York   10278

January 3, 1985

Comm. Hezekiah Brown
21 Truro Lane
Hempstead, New York   11550

Dear Hez:

Much to my own surprise, I feel no remorse about your leaving
FMCS. Of course, I will miss you as a friend and a colleague,
and FMCS will miss your outstanding work as a mediator, but
I am happy for you to move on to work that you expect to
find fulfilling and challenging. I hope you make the most
of your new opportunities.

You have been at the right place at the right time. The
labor-management community in the Metropolitan New York
area needed and was ready for a mediator of your skill
and devotion during the seventies and early eighties.

The environment FMCS provided gave you many opportunities
to learn the trade and to grow professionally. By learning
and growing, you achieved a high level of competence, and
demonstrated that there are no barriers that will not fall
to talent and character. Your activities have strengthened
FMCS in this community, and we are proud that we nurtured
you during your career with us. We wish you the greatest
success in your next career, and we look forward to continuing to work with you to promote peaceful solutions to the
inevitable conflicts in the labor-management community and
in the community at large.

Sincerely,

Paul Yager, Director, Eastern Region
FEDERAL MEDIATION & CONCILIATION SERVICE

NEW YORK STATE MEDIATION BOARD

Hezekiah Brown, Chairman of the New York State Mediation Board

The Buffalo News
By Joseph P. Ritz and Carolyn Racke
Thursday, February 15, 1990

STATE MEDIATION BOARD CHIEF GOT START HERE

Thursday was Hezekiah Brown's first day as the new Chairman of the State Mediation Board and he decided to spend it in Buffalo where, he said, "it all began."

The 51 year old Brown, who makes his home on Long Island, learned about labor negotiations as a shop committeeman and later President of United Auto Workers, Local 1173, representing workers at the former Chevrolet Tonawanda Foundry in the 1960's and early 1970's.

He became a Federal Mediator in 1972 in Buffalo before being transferred to the Federal Mediation and Conciliation Office in New York City. Thursday, Brown spent most of the day with Msgr. James Healey, who announced his resignation as Chairman last summer after 12 years in the position.

The new state mediation head was a pupil of Msgr. Healey when the priest taught at Cornell University State School of Labor and Industrial Relations here.

There is more of a need for Arbitration and Mediation now than ever before the Mobile, Alabama born Brown said.

Collective Bargaining has become more complex, "he said. "We find more social issues at the bargaining table than ever before, the whole issue of childcare, aid in the workplace…, drugs, drug testing, work sharing, health and welfare benefits. The issue of bereavement pay for animals, dogs, and cats. Some people are saying, "I don't have a child or a husband, so therefore, my family is my cat. Therefore, I should get bereavement pay."

"Some of the other issues reaching the negotiating table", Brown said, "are benefits for homosexual companions, flexible working hours and fitness plans in the workplace".

He sidestepped a question about his position on a suggestion made by some in state government to require those who use the state mediation and arbitration service to pay fees.

"I think it would be premature to comment on that the first day on the job", he said.

After 12 years as a Federal Mediator, Brown became Director of Labor-Management Programs at Cornell's School of Industrial and Labor Relations Extension in New York City. He also taught such subjects as Labor History and Conflict Resolution.

"I think I was born to do this kind of work," he said of his job as the state's top mediator. "It's really not work to me. I don't get tired because every case is a different challenge when you work in the field of arbitration and mediation, it's continuous growth. One of the things about mediation, every time you mediate, you not only mediate, you also teach the parties the process."

"There are times as a mediator," Brown recalled, "When you go into a room and notice that the animosity is so thick you can cut it with a knife. Then several days later, to be able to see those two people embrace, that's a great feeling."

After spending five years at Cornell University Extension, The Commissioner of Labor called and asked if I was interested in becoming the Chairman of the New York State Mediation Board. Again, I was honored and stunned to be offered this position. I remembered the night we had the discussion and I was asked if I would be interested in working in State Government. I replied that the only job in State Government that would interest me is serving as Chairman of the New York State Mediation Board. Surprisingly, that position became available and I accepted.

In 1990, I was nominated by Governor Mario Cuomo to serve as Chairman of the New York State Mediation Board, a statewide position with offices in Buffalo, Syracuse, Albany, New York City, and Long Island, New York. One of the final requirements was the confirmation process. I had to be confirmed by the Republican controlled Senate while the Governor was a Democrat. However, I was unanimously confirmed by the Senate. I was the first African American appointed to serve as Chairman in the history of over 100 years of existence.

I thought the hard part was over in getting the appointment and being confirmed. Little did I know that was the easy part! Upon my arrival to my New York City office, I was not greeted with open arms by the professional staff that was ALL white. There was a deep resentment that an African American had been appointed to this important position and the majority of the professional staff stated that they would NOT cooperate with me. They stated that nothing was going to change, and they would let me slowly twist away.

I quickly learned that the agency did not have a working fax machine and two copy machines that were inoperable. The entire office was actually dirty with coffee stains on the floor. A few of the staff had alcoholic problems, the walls were in dire need of painting and the staff was in violation of the law. The staff mediators and arbitrators were full time employees who were working outside of the agency for pay doing the same work they were supposed to be performing for free according to the New York State statute. They were supposed to be full time employees of New York state and providing arbitration and mediation as a free service from the state. However, they had developed a system where they were receiving full time pay from the state and had their arbitration business going at the same time. I called a meeting of the staff and informed them that I was appointed by the Governor and confirmed by the New York State Senate to be the Chief Administrator of this office and informed them that the office was dirty and the public was aware that dirty things were going on and needed to be corrected. Things would have to CHANGE. I heard smirks and snickers and saw the "no way" look on their faces.

It became apparent to me that talking to this group was not going to get it. I would have to do something BOLD to prove to them that I was serous about cleaning the office in both ways – staff and building.

After consultation with the various departments regarding hiring someone or having the maintenance clean the place up. I was informed that the State did not have any funds to buy carpet or paint the office. I know then that I would have to do what I know to do best! I went out and purchased paint and painting tools, and at the end of the day, I changed into my painting overalls and came in on Saturday and Sundays and initially painted the secretarial staff work area. The secretarial staff was delighted that I would paint their office first. That won them over while many of the professional staff made fun of me and consistently made jokes about my appointment and that the Governor had put me in a dungeon and nothing would change.

Shortly after I started to paint, two new fax machines and a copy machine arrived. I painted three large conference rooms because I wanted our clients coming into a clean area. I was informed by the Albany office that one of its agencies had ordered new furniture and in the interim period they were merged with another agency and the new furniture would be shipped to our offices. Just prior to the furniture being delivered, the State approved of new carpet for the entire office. The staff was baffled, and they start to acknowledge that maybe this guy has some connections!

We ultimately got the entire office painted and I again spent my money to purchase picture to put on the walls. In a relatively short time, the office looked professional. The support staff was absolutely delighted and started to come to work on time and perform their duties. They were inspired and happy to come in an office that was clean with all the machines working!

As budget time approached, all the department heads were informed by the Governor's staff that we must reduce our budget by 20%. I asked them if it would help if I reduced my budget by **30%!** They looked at me as though I was crazy! All the other agencies were complaining about cutting their budget and I was offering them more than they had asked. Finally, they asked me how I could cut my budget by 30%. I explained to them that we had an overabundance of supervisors and we could relieve all of them of their duties, I could manage the offices!

However, I could only implement my plans if it was supported firmly by the Governor because when the individuals learn what my plans were, they would run to the Governor to try and get me to reverse my decision. I was assured by the Governor that he would firmly support my plan, for which he DID! I was able to reduce supervisors in Buffalo, Syracuse, Albany, and New York City which was an enormous savings for the State. Incidentally, those supervisors who were reduced to mediator ultimately retired.

While serving as Chairman I implemented two programs to aid and assist the agency in carrying out its mission. I appointed an Advisory Committee consisting of labor and management representatives, arbitrator, mediators, and academies. They were appointed to advise the Board on labor relation matters. Another innovative and creative program I implemented was the Arbitration training program for individuals who wanted to become arbitrators. It was a free program because we used National Academy of Arbitrators trainers which reduced the cost of providing this free service

The National Academy of Arbitrators are encouraged to provide training for those individual desirous of becoming Arbitrators at no cost to the individuals. The program was good for the agency because it gave us additional individual to assist our agency in providing a free service to our clients.

I remained at the NYSMB for three years and returned to Cornell University Extension in New York City. My reason for returning to Cornell was due to the inability of the Governor to give pay increases due to budgetary problems and Cornell University wanting me to return. The other reason being I thought the Governor should have entered the Presidential race and I further believe he could have won. I expressed all of this to him in my letter of resignation.

In 1993, I returned to Cornell University Extension and picked up where I left off because my position was not filled while I was away. I continued to teach, train, and develop programs for the next six years. Upon my retirement from Cornell University Extension in 1999, I was presented with an Honorary PhD in Labor Studies for outstanding and innovative development of joint Labor-Management Programs.

UNIVERSITY OF BRIDGEPORT

While mediating a Labor Management dispute at the University of Bridgeport, I encountered two situations that should be noted.

The first incident happened during a heated exchange between the University Administration Negotiation Team and the American Association of University Professors (AAUP). The Chairman of the AAUP negotiation team was an Iranian who responded to the University by stating "we are not going to be the Niggers of the University." I was the only African American in the room, and everyone looked directly at me in embarrassment. However, instead of responding to his statement, I just ignored his statement and acted as if I did not hear his comments.

Subsequently, the parties requested a caucus. During the caucus, the Administration team showed signs of being embarrassed by what had happened and profusely apologized. I asked them what was the reason they were apologizing. They refused to state the reason for the apology because they wasn't sure I had heard what was said and they did not want to repeat it. I purposely continued to look puzzled regarding their apology and never acknowledged that I had heard the statement.

The AAUP team returned to the room and they started to apologize on behalf of their negotiation team in the same manner as the Administration. I again put my puzzled look on and acted as if I did not hear what the Chairman of the negotiation team had said. Then they began to look puzzled and question whether I had heard the remark. I explained to both parties that they were not talking to each other, they were talking at each other, and therefore, I wasn't listening to what was being said.

The Chairman of the Negotiation team finally realized that he had made a derogatory statement in the presence of a Federal Mediator and he too was embarrassed. At no point during the negotiations did I acknowledge that I had heard the remarks made by the Chairman.

At the conclusion of the negotiations, I was again quizzed regarding the statement. I finally confessed that I had heard the remarks and totally ignored what was said because my role as a Mediator was to assist the parties in reaching an agreement and definitely not become part of the problem. Had I reacted to the statement it would have had a devastating impact on the negotiations. The lesson learned and taught in this situation was the role of the mediator was not to react to a statement made by the parties but to stay focused on the mission of the Mediator.

The second incident that took place during these negotiations happened during the 7th week of the strike. The President of the University invited me to his home to have dinner with him and his wife. We had a wonderful dinner. As we concluded dinner, the President suggested that we retire to his study. As we began to discuss the impact of the strike, the President informed me that it was absolutely essential that we resolve this matter in an expeditious manner because the students were hanging out girls were being raped on campus and the parents were upset because the student were not in class. He was also concerned about the economic impact of the strike and the image of the University was being damaged, He stressed the urgency and importance of getting this matter resolved in the most expeditious manner possible. He asked me for suggestions.

I explained to him that due to the complexity of the issues, that it would be utterly impossible to reach a negotiated agreement. Therefore, we would have to do something different. I explained to him the possibilities of expanding the Mediation Team to include a panel of Mediators where I would serve as Chairman and the Administration would appoint a management professional to represent its' interest and the AAUP would appoint a Professional to represent its' interest. However, it would be a Mediation Team seeking to assist in resolving all issues.

The President of the University did not respond in a positive manner to my suggestion. However, the next morning, I saw the President on television recommending the appointment of a Mediation Panel to assist in resolving the strike. He detailed everything I had discussed with him as his recommendation to solve the strike and challenged the AAUP to join with him in accepting the recommendations. The AAUP accepted the President recommendation and they both appointed an individual to the panel and I served as chairman.

The Mediation Panel met with the parties for 27 straight hours and came up with a unanimous recommendation to the parties to end the strike at the University.

At the conclusion of the strike, and I was getting ready to return to New York, the President called me and asked me to stop by his office because he wanted to thank me for my efforts in resolving the dispute. During our conversation, he asked me if I knew how the strike got settled. I said yes and asked him how he thought it got settled. He asked me if remembered having dinner with him and his wife and going into his study after dinner. I again responded yes. He said that after I left his study, that he got on his knees and prayed to the good lord and asked him for a solution to this severe problem. He said the good lord gave him this idea regarding appointing a panel of Mediators to address the issues. I never responded to his version of his interpretation of the strike got resolved.

As a Mediator, one cannot take pride in authorship. The goal and objective is to render assistance and get the matter resolved and not look to take credit as long as the matter is resolved.

Our first major contract was with Consolidated Edison, the company that provided gas and electricity for New York and surrounding communities. Our company was awarded a contract for $2.1 million to train 14,000 employees in conflict resolution and diversity over two years because of an out of court settlement. The settlement consisted of a court order directing the company to train every employee in the company in conflict resolution and diversity. Upon receiving the contract, we hired and trained approximately 15 consultants to assist our company in meeting the goal directed by the company. We selected a diverse group of seasoned teachers and trainers and paid them $700.00 per day for training at various locations throughout the New York City area.

TRIP TO RUSSIA - 1992

I was in Russia from September 4, through September 15, 1992.

My purpose for traveling to Russia was to serve as one of nine instructors to teach approximately 150 Labor Officials who were members of the General Confederation of Trade Unions, The Moscow Federation of Trade Unions and other Independent Unions. Approximately 60% of the participants were Attorneys with the remaining being top Union Officials with many years of experience. I was the only African American on the team.

- Our task was to instruct the participants on five different topics.

- Communication Skills in Organizing

- Collective Bargaining in the Public and Private Sectors

- Contract Enforcement and Conflict Resolution

- Union Administration-Building Democratic Unions

- Labor Law and Political Action

The seminars were educational, interesting and thought provoking from two prospective, (1) It permitted me to examine, evaluate and compare our systems of problem solving with theirs. (2) It permitted the Russians to examine and evaluate our systems of Collective Bargaining.

My workshop went quite well and was non-controversial because the participants were interested in our systems of problem-solving through the grievance and Arbitration procedure. However, some workshops did not proceed along the same lines because the questions asked by the participant dealt more with the politics and practices of the AFL-CIO than the topics we were assigned to cover. Of course, the instructors differed vastly on the approach and verbally stressed it. I made my position crystal clear that I was not there as a politician, nor was I there to examine, criticize the AFL CIO policies toward the General Confederation of Trade Unions. We were able to overcome that obstacle quickly.

During my workshops, there was a great deal of interest in the following topics:

- What were the differences between the Taff Hartley Act and Collective Bargaining?

- What is the procedure for the enforcement of the collective bargaining agreement?

- Were employees permitted to make individual contracts with the employer?

- How to avoid strikes?

- Did the Unions have a legal right to strike?

- What extent is the Collective Bargaining Agreement binding?

- Is Arbitration binding on the parties?

- What is the role of mediators and are they effective?

- What legislative body is used to regulate the settlement of a labor dispute?

- There was a great deal interest in employee stock owned plans and joint ventures.

Since the topics we were teaching overlapped in some areas such as Collective Bargaining and Contract enforcement, we had to deal with extended questions on the two topics.

Additionally, The Participants showed a great deal of interest in our teaching technique. Therefore, James Miller and I conducted a workshop on How to train the trainer to which they were quite receptive and grateful

Other factors

The USSR originally consisted of approximately 270 million people. After the breakup, there were approximately 170 million in Russia and 100 within independent states or republics.

The Unions proudly pointed out that in the fall of the USSR, only two institutes survives: The Military and the Unions.

The General Confederation of Trade Unions which represent approximately 100 million workers is the old Communist Union and according to our information, there are a number of Independent Unions who represent another 70 million who will not affiliate with the GCTU.

POLITICS AND ENTREPRENEUR

Upon my retirement from Cornell University in January of 1999, I did two things. I started a family owned and operated business which consisted of my wife, comptroller son, president and daughter, Office Manager and myself CEO, Brown, Brown & Associates. It was a conflict resolution training center located in Hempstead, New York. Simultaneously, I entered the race for Trustee of the incorporated village of Hempstead.

Our first major contract was with Consolidated Edison, the company that provided gas and electricity for New York and surrounding communities. Our company was awarded a contract for $2.1 million to train 14,000 employees in conflict resolution and diversity over two years because of an out of court settlement. The settlement consisted of a court order directing the company to train every employee in the company in conflict resolution and diversity. Upon receiving the contract, we hired and trained approximately 15 consultants to assist our company in meeting the goal directed by the company. We selected a diverse group of seasoned teachers and trainers and paid them $700.00 per day for training at various locations throughout the New York City area.

POLITICAL CAREER

My political career started in Buffalo, New York in the 60's. I was involved in many first for African Americans in politics. I was involved in attempting to elect the first African American Mayor in Buffalo, New York, Ambrose Lane involved in electing the first African American Assembly person and the first African American Judge, Wilbur Trammel.

After being elected the youngest President of UAW, Local 1173 and subsequently appointed to the Federal Mediation and Conciliation Service, I left Buffalo, New York and ultimately move to Hempstead, New York. After arriving in Hempstead, New York, it was revealed that there was only one African American elected official in the Long Island community which consisted of approximately 3.5 million residents. He was registered Republican who once told me that he was Republican first and then black.

I started to work within the community and joined the Hempstead High School Vocational Educational Advisor committee under the leadership of Assistant Principal Gary Griggs. We did some phenomenal innovative and creative things on behalf of education. Initially we were trying to figure out how to extract funds from the various vendors who was doing business with the school district without causing a conflict of interest issue. In doing so we decided to implement a five-mile road race to raise funds for the High School Scholarship fund. Citi Bank had a community service who gave funds to various causes. Gary Griggs, the Assistant Principal at the high school and I met with the bank officials and they agreed to give us $5,000 for over five years to assist us in raising funds for scholarships. Essentially, they gave us $25,000 over five years which translated into over $50,000 in scholarships. We looked at the other methods to raise funds including creating programs for students such as implementing an Automobile Mechanic program at the high school. This program was primarily funded through grants and proposal writing. This program also assisted the community because citizens could bring their cars into the shop for tune-ups at no cost. We also offered car inspections at no cost to the residents. Created a print shop where students could learn the printing business and was guaranteed summer employment while saving the school district more than $30,000 a year. Received a $75,000 grant from Grumman Aerospace to create a machinist program. Students were eligible for a summer job at Grumman, and upon completion of the machinist program, they were guaranteed a job at Grumman's. We were instrumental in getting stoves donated by Brooklyn Union Gas Company for the home economics program and cars and minor damaged cars and trucks donated by General motors for the auto mechanic shop. In addition, we had a job bank in the high school. If an employer needed students for summer jobs, they could call the high school. Additionally, my Colleague Commissioner Robert Swanson and I assisted and encouraged the Hempstead High School to implement a Labor Relations course in the high school at almost no cost to the school district. We provided all of the instructors at no cost to the school district the only requirement of the school district were to supply a teacher to schedule the speakers were Labor-Management Practitioners, Arbitrators, Mediators, Labor-Management Specialists, Attorneys, College Professors. This was by far one of the most creative projects ever created because it exposed the high school students to a profession that they never have been exposed to. At the beginning of the school year, Commissioner Swanson and I selected a labor and a management collective bargaining team of student who were enrolled in the labor relations course and give them traditional collective bargaining issues and coached them in preparation for collective bargaining and actually negotiation a contract. The final collective bargaining was done before an assembly in the school auditorium. Negotiating before hundreds of students gave the process maximum exposure.

The essence of the program was felt by many because they were exposed to an unknown profession and learned about labor relations.

In learning about labor relations and Cornell University were instrumental in enrolling eleven student in four years from the Hempstead High School. Ten finished in four years and four went to law school.

SUPPORTIVE WIFE, CHILDREN, AND FAMILY

Hezekiah & Zelma Christine Brown

I have been married to the same wonderful, understanding, forgiving, loving, supportive, outstanding mother, grandmother, compassionate woman for 64 years. Her name is Zelma Christine Brown. We met in 1958 and married on April 23 1960, while we were very young. The only thing we knew is that we were in love and wanted to spend the rest of our lives together. We danced to an old love song "Love Is a Many Splendored Thing" recorded by Andy Williams and The Four Aces. The words in this song are so profound and beautiful, they capture the true feeling when you meet someone and fall in love.

This song explains how many young and elderly couples feel when they first meet and fall in love. They really believe that "love is a many splendored thing" and they truly believe that they really love each other, until they have their first child and first financial crisis. Apparently, something happens to that love is a many splendored thing! In fact, the blame game starts which creates unsolvable simple misunderstanding. In most instances, the parties are unable to deal with unforeseen problems because they are inexperienced in dealing with problems and end up finger pointing at each other and end up in divorce court. They fail to take advantage of anger and the far-reaching negative implications of refusing of failing to understand the humanistic part of conflict. It is okay to get angry and have conflict, because "making up" is wonderful, relaxing, and emotional.

In our case, the method in which we met is rather unique. I met her sister (Dorothy) at a dance prior to meeting her (Zelma). In the meantime, her sister (Dorothy) met my sister (Theresa). My sister explained to Dorothy that I was a "little bit wild" and needed someone to slow me down. Dorothy and Theresa concluded that Zelma was the one that could slow me down. Subsequently, Dorothy invited me to her Aunt's house, because I was a good dancer and so was Zelma. The night I met Zelma, we started to dance and danced all night and have been dancing since we first met.

In fact, many individuals predicted that we would not remain married for an extended period of time because we were and still are two different people. I was outgoing and enjoyed people, played sports too long, worked long hours and continue to be active in my community.

She is just the opposite, she did not understand sports, never joined any professional organizations or Sororities. She remained the same. However, she became active in Church and was ordained a Deaconess in the African Methodist Episcopal Zion Church.

In April 23, 2024, we will be married for 64 wonderful years (not dancing too much) but we still have a great relationship. We readily accepted the fact that we were different and learned to live with our differences and quickly learned the importance of respect for each other. In addition, we learned other valuable lessons that contributed to our successful marriage. We learned early about the art of forgiving, apologizing, compassion, compromising, allowing for mistakes and acknowledging that no one is perfect. Finally, the most profound thing we learned that still works for us today is; "Every statement does not require a response".

The Brown Family
Hez, Chris, Rodney, Chandra

It was only by the grace of God, a loving and devoted wife, Zelma Christine, and mother of our children Rodney and Chandra, and an exemplary supportive family, Roberta, Margaret, Theresa, Doris, Willie, Ann, Cozy, Paula, Nathaniel, Ann, Johnnie (deceased), Sammie, Tommie, Bettie, and numerous extended family members, David, Dorothy, Willie Elma, Tyrone and Irene.

My family was and continues to be extremely proud of me and the things that I have accomplished by navigating this complicated system to reach some of the top and most powerful positions in the country. There are others in this wonderful family who also took advantage of what is offered in this great country of our and became successful authors, educators, managers, supervisors, and entrepreneurs. We continue to stay close as a family and with the same spirit of our love, respect, and support for each other. We all continue to believe that we are a blessed family by showing appreciation through God and sharing our talents and blessing with the communities throughout the United States. To God be the glory for all the things He has done.

Rodney L. Brown

City of Buffalo
Executive Chamber
Proclamation

On behalf of the Citizens of the City of Buffalo,
I hereby extend congratulations and best wishes to

Hez and Christine Brown

on the occasion of their

50th Wedding Anniversary

WHEREAS, Hez and Christine Brown have spent 50 years in sacred union and devotion to each other, growing in love and recognition and, at the same time, giving of themselves not only to their family, but also contributing to improve the quality of life for the entire Buffalo community; and

WHEREAS, Hez and Christine Brown were married on April 23, 1960 and have been blessed with two children, Rodney and Chandra.

NOW, THEREFORE, BE IT RESOLVED THAT I, BYRON W. BROWN, Mayor of the City of Buffalo, do hereby proclaim April 23, 2010 as

Hez and Christine Brown Day

in the City of Buffalo and extend our congratulations and best wishes for continued health and happiness.

IN WITNESS WHEREOF, I have hereunto set my hand and caused the Seal of the City of Buffalo to be affixed this 23rd day of April, 2010

BYRON W. BROWN
MAYOR

Hezekiah Brown

CELEBRATING THE GOALS & ACHIEVEMENTS OF HEZEKIAH BROWN

Background, Views and Agenda of Hezekiah Brown

A LEADER AND A STATESMAN

Hezekiah Brown is widely recognized as one of the nation's foremost mediators and experts in conflict resolution. A resident of Hempstead, Hez has often been called upon by top leaders of the nation and the world to defuse potentially dangerous crises. Through his natural people-sense, specialized training, and years of experience, Mr. Brown has developed the unique and wonderful ability to bring angry combatants together to achieve common goals. From an in-born concern for people and their needs, and through long years of training and experience, Hezekiah Brown has emerged as a man who is both an effective leader and skillful statesman.

As a **leader**, Hez possesses the ability to transform the Hempstead political process into a continuous forum in which all residents are heard, in which all residents share participation in the decision-making, and in which all residents share in the economic and social benefit that come to the Hempstead community.

As a **statesman**, Hez is an able spokesman for the interests expressed by most Hempstead residents. He is a consummate master at advocating and promoting the realization of our community's goals and interests. Most important, however, he listens to residents and creates frequent opportunities for individual Hempstead residents to express their concerns, not only to himself, to each other.

Leadership and statesmanship are both are rare qualities, each of which plays a crucial role in the fate of communities and entire nations. Mr. Hezekiah Brown possesses a high degree of both qualities.

ALL THE WORLD LOVES A WINNER

Particularly in Hezekiah's service to his country, we see the bitter-sweetness of a young man who has been eager to serve his country, and, in so serving, has been given the opportunity to become much more that he had ever dreamed of becoming.

Hez has always focused on the positive aspect, but there has also been another aspect, the nagging bitterness of never quite getting the rewards that one deserves, of always being pulled away just when the benefits were about to be distributed

Many have walked away bitter and discouraged from such negative treatment, but Hez has taken it in stride, always managing to turn pending defeat into the final victory. The difficulties have made him an exceptional human being, one who can see a universality in human suffering, but who can also find a path to victory. Hez has always learned from any experience and used that knowledge to create success, not just for himself, but for everyone around him.

Victims may be despised, but *the entire world loves a winner!*

COMING DOWN THE HARD WAY

Hezekiah Brown served in the United States Army as a paratrooper in the 327 Airborne Battle Group. There he earned his *Parachutist Badge* after making five (5) qualifying jumps from an aircraft. He also eared the *Good Conduct Medal* and was promoted to specialist 4th class. Brown served as a squad leader, prior to being honorably discharged.

Hez says that *challenges are just a part of life.* In the life of a successful person, challenges are just opportunities to achieve victories.

Hez met his life's first real challenge when the Army asked him to jump out of an airplane. At first, he did not think that he could do it. He had not even been in an airplane prior to his first jump. As it turned out, he met the challenge and made 12 successful jumps before he finally landed in an airplane.

HEZ BROWN, THE SOLDIER

In Hezekiah Brown's military service, we see something of the bitter-sweet essence of being Black in America – the opportunities for growth, such as nowhere else in the world, and the ever-nagging discrimination which has defeated so many bright stars. Hez has never allowed that discrimination to defeat or discourage him. So, he has become a shining role model for excellence.

SUCCESS IN THE MILITARY

He learned at an early age that hard work and good choices really pay off. His choice of enlisting in the army at an early age set the stage for many other early successes.

Hez excelled in rank while in the service of his country, being promoted acting sergeant, specialist 4th class and squad leader. Yet, he also excelled in other activities, such as sports. He was an outstanding baseball player, playing on the 327th Airborne Battle Group's baseball and football teams.

TAKING ADVANTAGE OF MILITARY BENEFITS

Although Hez entered the military as a high school dropout, he was able to take advantage of many opportunities for education made possible by the military, both during and after active duty service. Not only did Hez receive many kinds of training, while on active duty, he continued his education after active duty under the *GI Bill,* earning two college degrees. He also purchased his first home under the *GI Bill* and used the veteran points offered by the federal government to qualify for entry as a federal mediator.

Hez speaks of his time in the US Army with fond passion, especially of the sound leadership skills that he developed in the process. However, it was not all fun and games. Hez helped to make history, while on active duty.

For instance, Hez was one of the soldiers to help to accomplish the first integration of a previously all-White school in the nation, Central High School in Little Rock, Arkansas. The President of the United States ordered US Army troops to guard the *Little Rock Nine* and bring these little, Black children safely to class, integrating Central High School. The 327th Airborne Battle Group was the first unit to arrive in Little Rock for this duty. Hez said that he felt immensely proud to be able to advocate for his people. Although, African Americans were not permitted to participate directly in guarding the school, Hez remained at the site for an extended period and was able to witness government in action –both the negative and the positive.

SEEING RICHNESS IN DIVERSITY

The year 2001 is certain to be a year of crisis for the people of the Village of Hempstead. Already, the new century is testing our community as never before. If the community is to prosper, it must make the best use of all its resources, both human and material. Hezekiah Brown has the vision, understanding and people-skills to lead a community renaissance and make Hempstead one of the foremost communities in the nation.

Hezekiah sees richness where others only see differences. Hezekiah sees opportunity where others only see problems. Hezekiah sees ability and skills where others only see unconventionality. Most important, Hezekiah has the skills and abilities to bring all the people, resources, and opportunities together to make *visions into realities.*

Hempstead is radically different from the ethnically uniform communities that surround it. While surrounding communities are much richer in affluence, Hempstead is rich in ethnic diversity. It is one of the few places on Long Island where new immigrants and Minorities are welcome. Its residents are united more by their common hopes for the future, than by a common language, a common religion, or any other common cultural attribute.

Hempstead could quickly become bogged down by social problems, or quickly buoyed up by industry and ingenuity. Whether its fate will be positive or negative will be determined mostly by its choice of leaders and the visions that those leaders will be superimposed upon it.

If the community chooses leaders, like Hezekiah Brown, that fate will surely be bright and happy. Hezekiah is a man of vision and human feeling who puts people first. For him, the beautiful village is the one in which the residents can feed and provide for their families in a safe and wholesome environment.

A TIME FOR EXCEPTIONAL SKILLS

Hempstead has many knowledgeable and talented residents, varying across a spectrum from well-established European-American families to upwardly mobile African American homebuyers; from Arab and East Indian shopkeepers to Dominican and Salvadoran Bodegas; from West Indian and Latin realtors to Jamaican and Ecuadorian day laborers. In the streets, one is almost as likely to hear Spanish, French or Korean as he is likely to hear English. Yet for all these people – hard working, family-loving and thrifty – the common denominator is their hopes of the future. That future will only exist for any one of them or any group of them if they can all come together and create a positive and productive environment for all of them. That requires a leadership which encompasses them all.

There are few people alive today who have Hezekiah's ability to get people to talk together, join hands, and derive a common agenda: an agenda which takes into account all of the needs of every member of the community and leaves no one out. Without such an agenda, those who want to help the community will only continue to squander our very meager opportunities.

Our community agenda is something which only we can derive. We will do this by holding forums in which we will all be able to speak our minds as individuals and be heard by every other member of our community. Most important, we must be empowered through our leaders to turn our agenda into a community program.

Thus, we must have leaders who are not afraid to allow us to speak our minds, and who have the commitment to us to act as executives of our common will, once that will be determined. Our leaders must be willing to act as our mediators and emissaries – to go out into the world and make our influence felt. Too often our leaders do just the opposite, becoming our jailers and oppressors, rather than our representatives.

The difference is that Hezekiah has the commitment to act for us all and the skills to bring us all to common action.

FORMING THE HEMPSTEAD CONSENSUS

We must all be heard, so that we can form a consensus, a single agenda that we can all fervently support. Then, our community will act as one, with unified spirit and determination, to meet the challenges ahead.

That wonderful consensus is possible, but through a process of continuous dialogue, mediated by skillful leaders. Only in a carefully controlled process of mediation and conflict resolution may all our various hopes and dreams be welded together into a common cause, our consensus.

However, there are only a small number of individuals who possess that amazing combination of mediation and leadership skills. Hempstead is incredibly lucky to possess one such individual in Hezekiah Brown. As we face the uncertainties of Year 2001, we need to make sure that we make the very use of him.

MANY ARE CALLED, BUT HEZEKIAH HAS WHAT IT TAKES

Hempstead is blessed with many individuals who have the ambition and courage of conviction to step forward. Some have already answered the call to leadership, but few possess the leadership and mediation skills that are possessed in abundance by Mr. Hezekiah Brown.

Hezekiah Brown has an absolute commitment to the integrity and growth of the Hempstead Community, but he also has something more. His vision includes the prosperity of every Hempstead resident – rich or poor; Black, brown, or white; English speaking or non-English speaking: employee, manager, or entrepreneur. Most important, Hezekiah Brown can bring all of Hempstead's people together to make that prosperity happen for all.

Promoting the Integrity of His Community

NO MIRACLES, JUST RESULTS

Hezekiah & Rodney Brown with Senator Chuck Schumer

Once the highest-ranking African American in New York State government, Hezekiah Brown is the former commissioner of the NYS Board of Arbitration. However, the confidence which state and national leaders have placed in Hez tells only a portion of his story.

Perhaps, a more revealing measure of the man is shown in Hez' commitment to maintain the integrity of his community, and the esteem which that commitment has earned him from his fellow residents of the Village of Hempstead.

Hez Brown is a family man, married to the same wife, Christine, for forty years. Together, they raised a successful son and daughter, respectively, Rodney and Chandra. These two children have brought them a daughter-in-law, Maxine; and two granddaughters, Crystal and Chanee.

The pride and importance which Mr. Brown has placed in family extend to his neighborhood and community. His concerns, as a family man, have led to his concerns as a member of the Hempstead community.

Concern for his community has been a priority for Hezekiah Brown. No matter how involved he has become on the state and national levels, he has always made time for his family, neighborhood, and village.

While successfully mediating some of the thorniest labor disputes in recent history, he found time to spend three years as a highly active member of the Hempstead Board of Education. During his tenure, he won wide acknowledgment for his efforts to focus the resources of the Hempstead School District upon the children.

One of the students made a positive observation regarding the work of Assistant Principal Gary Griggs and Hezekiah Brown: She stated that Mr. Griggs and Mr. Brown was a "tag team." Mr. Griggs was on the inside helping students and Mr. Brown was on the out side. Great team.

Some of their Accomplishments in the school district have included initiating the Hempstead School District Hall of Fame, helping it initiate and acting as co-chair of the Hempstead High School Scholarship Road Race and chairing the Hempstead High School Vocational Education Committee.

Hez has helped to develop a labor relations course at Hempstead High School and has directly assisted many Hempstead High School students in gaining admission to Cornell University.

Most notable, they helped persuade the Grumman Aerospace Corporation to grant Hempstead High School $75,000 for its Machinist Program.

In local politics, Hez has served as Hempstead Zone Leader for the Democrats. At one time, he served as a key fund-raiser for five-term Assembly member, Earlene Hooper-Hill.

One indication of Hez' sense of priorities was shown in the advice and grooming which he provided a decade ago to long-time friend and fellow church board member, James A. Garner. In spite of the fact that Mr. Garner was a Republican, Hez joined many other Democrats in helping to get Mr. Garner elected as the Village of Hempstead's first African American mayor. In the hope that having a mayor from the community would give community members greater access to community resources, Hez put friendship and community need above party affiliation.

Hez has remained proud of spirit of what that election, long ago, has accomplished for the community, although man elected has not proved true to that spirit.

Hez has also served as chairman of the Hempstead Neighborhood Advisory Council, a state-funded organization which brought together many kinds of community service organizations into one, coordinated effort to uplift the Village of Hempstead.

Hez has recently been elected as Trustee of the Village of Hempstead, with Wayne Hall, one of the first two Democrats elected to that board in recent history. Hez and Wayne have already given government a new openness and responsiveness to community which have been lacking in the Village of Hempstead for more than two decades.

Hez' other local affiliations include: membership on the board of directors, Nassau County Girl Scouts of America; membership on the board of directors, Operation Get Ahead, Inc.: member of the Hempstead Branch, NAACP; member of the United Neighbors Civic Association; and member of the Jackson Memorial A.M.E. Zion Church (Hempstead).

The success of Hez' local efforts have been applauded by some of the most powerful and prestigious organizations in the area. Most notably, the Hempstead Branch of the NAACP has presented him with its *Person of the Year Award*, and Hofstra University has presented in its *Unispan Award*.

Most notable, Cornell University presented Hez with an honorary *Doctorate in Labor-Management (Ph.D.)*.

Less prestigious, but just as indicative of the affection with which Hez is revered in the community, the Marguerite Golden Rhodes Elementary School (Hempstead) presented him its *Dr. Martin Luther King, Jr. Humanitarian Award*.

HEZEKIAH BROWN, MEDIATOR, PAR EXCELLENCE

A veteran arbitrator and mediator, Hezekiah Brown has developed his skills in the field of industrial and labor relations for more than 25 years. He is now one of the foremost authorities in his field. His expertise is being sought by top administrators on the state and national level, as well as by academicians.

Hez has just recently retired as director of one of the nation's most-widely recognized college courses on *conflict resolution:* The Labor-Management Program at the School of Industrial and Labor Relations, Cornell University.

However, from 1990 until 1993, he served as New York State's top mediator: Chairman of the New York State Employment Relations Board, directing offices in Albany, Buffalo, Hempstead, Hauppauge, Syracuse, and New York City. He was the first African American to hold his cabinet-level position, and, at the time, was one of the highest-ranking African American in New York State government.

WIDELY RECOGNIZED FOR HIS STATESMANSHIP

A few years ago, former U. S. Secretary of Labor Robert Reich appointed Hez to serve on a government task force to evaluate nation labor relations policy in the public sector.

This was not the first time Hez' abilities were recognized by national leadership. In 1983, Hez received recognition from the Republican side of the political aisle, as President Ronald Reagan presented him with *Presidential Recognition Award* for Community Service.

Then in 1992, Hez was chosen to assist the Russian nation with its transition to a market economy. He was sent to that county to teach *conflict resolution* and *contract administration.*

Again in 1992, Hez served as chief mediator for the Democratic National Convention. Afterwards, he was highly praised for keeping peace between labor and management during that historic convention.

A DIFFICULT ROAD TO THE TOP

Hez has earned his state and national recognitions after many years of hard work on the grassroots level. He first gained public attention in 1970 when he was elected president of UAW Local 1173, the youngest person to hold that position. Having completed his Bachelor's in *Labor Relations* at Empire State College and his advanced studies in mediation and labor relations at Cornell, Hez developed into a skilled negotiator, winning many favorable contracts for his local union and wide acclaim for his abilities.

Two years later (1972), Hez' reputation as a negotiate had grown to the point that he was appointed as a commissioner for the Federal Mediation and Conciliation Service, making history as the youngest African American to be so appointed. He served that agency for 12 years, resolving many historic labor disputes throughout the New York Metropolitan Area, the Virgin Islands, and Puerto Rico.

In all, Hez has personally resolved more than 2,000 significant labor and community disputes.

In his capacity as chairman of the State Mediation Board, Hez mediated settlements in some of the hottest labor disputes of our times, disputes that have drawn headlines and extensive media coverage. There have included Consolidated Edison and the utility workers; the Brooklyn Union Gas and the Transport Workers Unions; the Sanitation Workers and the International Brotherhood of Teamsters Union; the New York Post and the newspaper unions; the New York Ethical and Cultural School and the Independent Union; Schweizer Aircraft and the United Auto Workers, and Local 1199 and various hospitals.

Mr. Brown is a member of the Society of Professionals in Dispute Resolution. He is a founder and past president of the Industrial Relations Research Association.

For his many regional and national successes, Hez has received many awards, among which are the *Black Achievers in Industry Award,* and the *Public servant of the Year Award* from Queens College. He is also listed in *Who's Who in Labor* and featured in a book written to inspire American youth across the country, *100 African American Professionals.*

Putting It Together for People
NO MIRACLES; JUST RESULTS

As one of the Nation's foremost experts in mediation and conflict resolution, Hezekiah Brown is highly accomplished in the skills and techniques that bring divergent groups and factions to the table – not only to resolve conflicts and disputes, but also to join together in support of political issues, to create important community efforts, and to achieve collective economic successes.

Hezekiah's Community Involvement has included:

1. Currently serves as Hempstead Village trustee
2. Former member, Hempstead Board of Education
3. Former Co-Chairman, Hempstead High School Scholarship Road Race
4. Former chairman, Hempstead High School Vocational Education Committee
5. Former chairman, Hempstead Neighborhood Advisory Committee
6. Board member, Operation Get Ahead
7. Former president, Hempstead Coordination Council
8. Former vice president, United Neighborhood Civic Association'
9. Former chairman, Hempstead for Hofstra Scholarship Committee

Hez has shown an exceptional ability to bring people together who, in many cases, do not even talk to each other. This skill is especially important, right ow when the people of Hempstead are greatly divided by language, political philosophies, and countries of origin. However, Hez knows that the people of Hempstead have much more in common than they have differences. Hez knows that all the residents have come here seeking a better life for themselves and their families, and that all are willing to work hard to achieve that goal. He will provide the leadership to get all segments of the community working together, to achieve that goal, not only for individuals and family, but for the entire Hempstead community. He has the skills and understandings to achieve that but getting all to participate in creating and profiting from a better Hempstead.

Hez says, "No miracles; just results!"

A BRIEF LOOK AT HEZEKIAH BROWN

Hezekiah Brown is president of Brown, Brown & Associates, Inc., and the recently retired director of Labor-Management Programs at Cornell University's New York State School of Industrial and Labor Relations.

Over the past years, Hez has served as arbitrator, mediator and negotiator for both management and labor, including 12 years as commissioner of the Federal Mediations and Conciliation Service.

Hez served as New York State's chief mediator and as chairman of the New York State Employment Relations Board, one of New York State's highest ranking African American official.

As an instructor, he has designed and developed *labor-management* and *quality of working life* programs and has done extensive work in the areas of *conflict resolution* and *labor-management cooperative programs,* including mediation of over 400 labor disputes and numerous domestic and community conflicts.

In September 1992, Hez was selected as one of 10 instructors to visit Russia to teach *contract administration* and *conflict resolution* to the Russians as they began the transition to a market economy.

DEMOCRATIC TRUSTEES FORCE MAYOR TO SHARE URBAN RENEWAL INFORMATION WITH RESIDENTS

By Trustee Hezekiah Brown

I believe that the Village government should be an open government that encourages individuals to participate in the governmental process, rather than a government of exclusion, such as we continually witness in the Village of Hempstead. Government is supposed to be responsible to the resides and taxpayers. However, our Village government can be interpreted as being a government of exclusion because many important decisions that are decided which have direct impact on the residents are made without valuable input from the residents.

As most of you know, the Urban Renewal project that is taking place in our Village has been in the process for over ten years. Yet, most residents and businesspeople are neither aware of the economic aspects of it, nor the impact it will have on them.

SUPPORTS REAL
ECONOMIC DEVELOPMENT

Just to set the record straight, Wayne Hall and I are not opposed to real economic development. However, we are opposed to the method used by Republican/Unity Party. They are withholding valuable information from residents and businesses that are directly impacted by the Urban Renewal plan.

We believe that the government should be your ally, as opposed to being perceived as your enemy. We further believe that information should be flowing on a daily (or as needed) basis to those individuals affected by the Urban Renewal plan, instead of those individuals being kept in suspense. We should be informing the residents of our village of the impact that economic development and Urban Renewal is having on small business tax base and schools. We should be informing them on the long- and short-range plans for other economic development. If we do not bring residents with us, we may find ourselves with two large shopping malls and the rest of our downtown deserted.

Are there other plans to further develop the rest of our Village? We believe that there should be on-going dialogue between Village officials and residents when the future of the Village is at stake. We further believe that the Village officials should visit all segments of the community, rather than demand that all meetings be held at Village Hall, as we witnessed recently.

HEMPSTEAD'S PRESENT ADMINISTRATION DISREGARDS PEOPLE

On August 10, 2000, individuals who were directly impacted by the Urban Renewal project requested that the Mayor meet with them and members of ACORN at the Hempstead Lutheran Church. They particularly wanted officials from the Village and the Hempstead Community Development Agency to explain how the of the United States Housing and Urban Development Department's rules and relations and regulations on relocation applied to them. However, the May refused to appear at the church. Instead, he wrote an article in the *Hempstead Beacon* accusing Wayne Hall and I of *"playing politics."*

Unlike our Republican/Unity Party colleagues, Wayne Hall and I attended the meeting at the Church, because we firmly believe that Village officials should share information with residents at whatever location is most effective and best reaches residents, particularly those residents who are most adversely affected. We believe that some meetings should be held in the affected areas, to maximize the participation of the community.

As *Newsday* has already reported, Mayor Garner had told Wayne Hall that he would attend the meeting at the Church. However, at the last minute, he apparently changed his mind. He then demanded that the meeting take place at Village Hall. Residents were legally entitled to that information. Yet, the mayor said that anyone who wanted information could get it there or not get it at all.

It is my humble opinion that the Mayor grossly erred when he refused to attend a meeting requested by the community. These residents were legally entitled to receive specific information regarding relocation.

Finally, the Republican/Unity Party trustees very seldom visit village neighborhoods, unless they are issuing political citations, like their political counterpart, Nassau County Executive Thomas Gulotta.

Wayne Hall and I believe that Village officials should visit every segment of the community periodically, instead of sitting at Village Hall and demanding that every meeting he conducted there.

Remember, *"You, can fool some of the people all of the time; and you can fool all of the people some of the time. However, you can never fool all of the people all of the time!"*

ELIZABETH CITY'S GAIN, HEMPSTEAD'S LOSS

Hezekiah Brown and Christine Brown

To experience loss is as much a natural part of life as life itself. Some losses, however, are more profound than others. Take the loss of two of Hempstead's quintessential solid citizens, Hez and Chris Brown via relocation to Elizabeth City, North Carolina. Never have two people impacted the lives of so many, including this writer, than Hez and Chris Brown. And never will two people be so missed by so many, Not to say that life will not go on, because it usually does not matter how great the loss. But to say that life in Hempstead will be the same without them is, as the old folk used to say, a lie and the truth ain't in 'em. More than just a metaphor, Hez and Chris Brown were indeed the life of the party, figuratively and literally. Their friendly home was often the center of the political and social world of Nassau County. It was there where warm dinners with family and close friends took place. It was the home of Hez and Chris Brown where Nassau County Democratic reformers incubated and hatched much of the strategy that led to Roger Corbin being elected as the first black democrat to the incoming county legislator. It was there where much of the plans were laid for takeover of party leadership and county government. Needless to say, there was much success in all three endeavors. It was also where those seeking public office sought Hez's counsel and advice. It was the place where Hez helped friends and enemies alike who were seeking employment or positions in county government; where many of us including this writer and others were political and financial beneficiaries from being around Hez and Chris Brown; where for the first time many of us met seasoned and budding stars in the political arena; where joyous holiday parties, fun-filled Bar-B-Qs and spirited table-slapping whiz playing took place. This was the spot where the best darn party in town were held. And if you are lucky enough to be there when the Browns partied you know you have witnessed the mother of all parties. This was also the home where Mr and Mrs Brown and her family unselfishly and with open arms bestowed unconditional love as if you were family; where some of us, including this writer needed an encouraging word, a kind deed, or someone just to listen to self-absorbed gripes and petty complaints Mr and Mrs Brown were there. Although Hez graciously appeared to be giving you a sympathetic ear, Mrs. Brown seemed a little less sympathetic. She had no problem giving you the proverbial swift kick in the you-know-what, that told you to climb down off that pity wagon and do something for yourself. Their love and caring for others went beyond the confines of their friendly home. When one of their friends is hospitalized and in need of a friendly smile or a pick-me-up bedside quip Hez provided the joke and Christine offered the friendly smile. The point is, Hez and Christine Brown were always there. This is what Elizabeth City has gained and what Hempstead has lost.

So the optimum question is what manner of people are Mr. and Mrs Brown? What is it that shaped the exemplary character and values of Hez and Chris Brown.

Well the story, at least for Hezekiah Brown began on June 21, 1938, in the small rural town of Prichard, Alabama. He is the third child and the eldest son of eleven children born to Carrie and Sam Brown. When Hez Brown talks about his humble beginnings he is just not talking about abstract poverty, but poverty with a capital P. With what he calls good luck and being blessed, his biography that now reads like a Horatio Alger's Rags to Riches story would need more space than what is allowed here. Hez had his first job at age six chopping wood in a wood yard. He also worked the fields digging potatoes. When Hez became a little older he would accompany his father along with some of his brothers travel mostly on a flatbed truck to Florida and Virginia for jobs as migrant field workers. One summer, after working the fields in Cheriton Virginia, his boss took them farther north to East Bethany in upstate New York which is about fifty miles outside of Buffalo. They went there to do similar type of work, but the conditions and times were unbelievably tough for Hez. He often went hungry and at one point slept in a barn. Things were so bad that when his older sister Theresa, who was living in Buffalo at the time, came to visit him she wept. She returned about a week later and after packing his meager personal affects in two paper bags she took Hez home with her. After working at General Motors assembly plant for about four months he joined the U. S. Army at age 18 and was assigned to the 101" Airborn Paratroopers. It was his unit that then President Eisenhower deployed to the racial hotbed of the capital city of Little Rock Arkansas to protect, who had become internationally and nationally known, the brave Little Rock Nine. Originally Hez had intended to make the armed forces a lifetime career. But after being advised that he should pursue a professional baseball career, because he was pretty good at hitting the ball, Hez was discharged from the army following a two year stint. Hez' defensive ability was not on par with his hitting skills and thus had to abandon his dream of becoming a professional baseball player. Hez returned to General Motors and his wise sister knew that Hez needed a more grounded life style. She had the right person in mind to settle him down and introduced him to a pretty brown skin level headed 17 year old young lady by the name of Zelma Christine Harper. Hez had the good sense not to let her get away and he and Christine from Camden New Jersey were married on April 23, 1960. Hez says that marrying Chris was the best move he ever made. She is from a family of 12 children and Hez being from the clan of 11 siblings extended Hez and Chris' family considerably especially since the two of them are truly big on family. With Hez and Chris such family include their church family and close friends whom they refer to as their extended family. There is no question that the merging of the Browns and the Harpers seem to have worked well for both family units and members of their extended family.

Hez and Chris bought their first home when he was 21 and 1961 they were Blessed with their first child Rodney and three years his sister Chandra was born. They both now run the family business. Meantime, Hez was speaking out about poor working conditions at the General Motors plant which made him a hit with fellow workers. Because of his, as he says, "big mouth" Hez was elected by his older co-workers as shop steward with UAW Local 1177. At age 23, he was the youngest person in the history of the local to ever hold that position. Not satisfied with just talking about working conditions Hez went on to set another milestone. Through his work as shop steward Hez was instrumental in the creation of an in-house AAA Program for workers at the GM plant. What he is most proud of, however, was his research and written report about specific job-related illnesses such as silicosis caused by poor air quality, hearing problems due to constant high noise levels within the plant and stress-related hypertension (high blood pressure) Union officials were so impressed about his findings and particularly the quality and effort that went into the report, Hez was summoned to Detroit to present the report to top UAW Bosses. Because of his hard work and dedication to his job, Hez quickly began a meteor-like rise up the ladder of success in both his professional and personal life.

As it relates to his illustrious work career over a thirty-five-year period in the field of labor relations, Hez has been an arbitrator, mediator and negotiator for management and labor. This also included 12 years as Commissioner with the Federal Mediation and Conciliation Service. Related to those endeavors he was Project Director for the Minority Arbitrator's Training Program partly sponsored by Cornell University and Hofstra Law School. Hez has also been Chief Mediator and Chairman of member of Governor Cuomo's cabinet. His work has also afforded him the opportunity to travel outside of the U.S. to such places as Russia where he taught Contract Administration and Conflict Resolution and Europe to study the global application of labor- management Cooperation. Hez was also appointed by Robert Reich, former Secretary of Labor, to serve on the Labor Management Task Force for Excellence in State and Local Government through Labor Management Cooperation. Hez taught the curriculum that he developed, Dispute Resolution Certificate Program at Cornell University; which attracted students from all over the U.S. as well as many others from several countries.

In the meantime, when Hez became a Federal Mediator, he moved his family from Buffalo to Queens, New York, in 1973, where they made lifelong friends. Four years later they bought a home in Hempstead. Also around that time Hez began to deeply involve himself in local politics. His first successful effort in the political arena was being part of a group Hempstead citizens that helped to elect the first African American mayor on Long Island. He was elected to the Hempstead School Board of Education, but his term was interrupted when he was tabbed by Cuomo to be part of his administration.

When Coumo's governorship ended Hez returned to Hempstead politics with gusto, primarily with the Democratic Party. After the failure of his first try as village Trustee, Hez ran a second time with success. After serving two years in that position Hez was appointed Deputy County Executive by Tom Souzzi, the newly elected County Executive. In giving it his all to help put the new county administration on the right track the burden of taking on everyone else's burden, the treasonous craziness that had taken hold of Hempstead politics and the many years of toil to make his family secure, fatigue and frustration had finally begun to take its toll on Hez. It was time to leave. Most of all, it was time for Hez to take care of the devoted lady who for the past 44 years has unflinchingly been by his side, through the good times and bad, wife, mother, grandma and AME Zion Deaconess, Z. Christine Brown. In her own right Chris Brown has also made a positive mark on humanity, especially children. She has personally taken other people's children under wing to tutor them and provide them with proper guidance. She has also been generous to those who might sometimes be in need of a little help to tide them over. This writer feels that one of Chris' proudest achievement was when she was ordained Deaconess of her former Hempstead Church. She has transferred her Deaconess Certificate to her new AME House of Worship.

TEACHING OUR CHILDREN TO COPE
By R. Hugo Adams

Our children are living a nightmare. They are enveloped in violence. They live in dread. They are distracted from meaningful pursuits. They are discouraged from personal enrichment. We want to awaken them to a fuller life, but first we have to awaken ourselves. There is a way, but that way is not simple.

Violence is all around us. It has become a frequent resort, a common means of coping. There seems no escape from the violence in our communities. Wherever we see people come into conflict, we see the horrible statistics increase.

One of the top mediators in the state of New York, Hezekiah Brown, has said, "Every time we read the newspaper or listen to the radio, we hear about some type of conflict that has gone awry. Young people are killing each other. Families are being torn apart. Ethnic groups are fighting each other; the list goes on.

He said, "As great as we are, we Americans, don't know how to deal with conflict. In a way, it's fascinating. We, Americans, are so advanced and skillful in technology, but we don't know how to deal with our neighbors. We solve our problems with power. We become overbearing. Instead of teaching our children how to solve problems, we teach them to create problems. We teach our children to hate people they don't even know. That's why there is so much racism."

He concluded, "Conflicts are an inevitable part of living in a society, but conflicts can be resolved, and without violence!"

SUFFER THE LITTLE CHILDREN

We know that our children are in trouble, perhaps more than any other recent generation. Our children are on the front line of American social conflict, especially our young, Black males. In recent years, the pistol has become the most frequent cause of death of African American males under the age of twenty-five.

Violence has become a fact of all our lives, and, for an increasing number of students in New York's public-school systems, violence has become a daily means of coping. The current extent of the resort to violence is indicated by the need to use metal detectors at many area high schools. Yet, metal detectors do not solve the problem. The violence occurs anyway. The problem is the "will" to do violence. Where there is a "will", there is a "way."

Putting the "blame" on a teacher, a principal or a superintendent and then firing her or him, may make us feel better, but it does little solve the problem. We keep wanting to push a button or "pop" a pill to make it all go away. But there is no button, and there is no pill, and there is no panacea. There is only understanding, and a procedure call conflict resolution. This procedure will help to make the situation better, but it is hard work.

CONFLICT RESOLUTION: A SKILL TO BE MASTERED

Conflict Resolution can be taught. It consists of a set of understandings and skills developed over several centuries by successful mediators and by dedicated researchers. The Cornell University School of Industrial and Labor Relations is a major depository of that knowledge and Hezekiah Brown is one of the products.

Now director of labor-management programs at Cornell, Mr. Brown completed his bachelor's in labor relations at Empire State College degree and went on to do advance studies in mediation and labor relations at Cornell. Drawing upon his many years as a union negotiator and later as a federal mediator, Brown recently served as New York State's top mediator, chairman of the New York State Employment Relations Board.

During his three years as chairman of this board, Mr. Brown negotiated settlements in some of the hottest labor disputes of the time, disputes whose importance was indicated by front-page headline and extensive media coverage: notably, Consolidated Edison and the utility workers; Brooklyn Union Gas and the Transport Workers Unions; the Sanitation Workers and International Brotherhood of Teamsters Union; the New York Post and the Newspaper Unions; the New York Ethical and Cultural School and the Independent Union; Schweizer Aircraft and United Auto Workers; and various hospitals and Local 1199.

His effectiveness as a resolver of conflicts has been recognized by such organizations as Queens College of Labor and Research which named him as Public Servant of Year 1992; and the National Democratic Convention committee, which praised his work as chief mediator charged with keeping peace between labor and management during the 1992 Democratic National Convention.

ACHIEVING POSITIVE RESULTS

Mr. Brown said, "Whenever human beings interact with other human beings, there is the potential for conflict. Conflict is inevitable when people's attitudes, values, goals, personalities, or expectations differ."

Specifically, he said, "Conflict occurs when two or more parties believe that what each want is incompatible with what the other wants. The 'parties' can be individuals, groups, organizations, or nations. Their wants may range from having an idea accepted to gaining control of a limited resource."

However, he has said that it is not the conflict itself, but how the parties go about trying to resolve the conflict which creates the problems. He said, "The manner in which you approach the conflict will determine whether you reach a positive outcome or continue the conflict."

Conflict resolution is not just a body of theory, but a skill, a technique. He said, "Mediation does not require a lot of theories. We learn it experientially. To become a conflict resolver, one begins with self-examination. That is the first lesson. It shows you how you look at others. To learn to resolve conflicts, you must learn to make the cross-over, to be able to understand the other side of the issue, even to be able to argue the other side of the issue."

He has said, "You bring prejudices and biases to every discussion. You have to learn to leave your baggage at home. You have to learn to listen. The more that you know about the person involved in a conflict, the easier it is to resolve that conflict."

FOCUSING ON THE NEED TO DEVELOP CONFLICT RESOLVERS

Brown said, "Conflict resolution is not a panacea, but it will ease the problem."

The "trick", he said, is to get people to understand that working with other people requires an investment of time and effort. He wants people to know that conflicts are inevitable whenever two or more individuals come together, but that positive resolution of those conflicts can also become the normal state of affairs.

Said Brown, "Dealing with conflict is a major management function in organizations today. A survey of top and middle managers suggests that they spend approximately 45% of their time dealing with conflict, and they consider the ability to manage conflict to be of increasing importance."

Brown, Brown & Associates

To focus upon the need to produce more conflict resolvers and to introduce conflict resolution as an integral component of public education, Mr. Brown has joined with other members of his family to Brown, Brown & Associates, a firm dedicated to resolving conflicts and teaching conflict-resolution skills. The principals of the firm are president, Mr. Brown; vice president, son, Rodney L. Brown and vice president, daughter, Chandra D. Brown.

Established in December 1992, the firm provides a framework for dedicated, full-time efforts to present conflict-resolution training courses to educators and other groups whose primary focus is people-to-people relations.

MAKING IN-ROADS IN THE VIOLENCE

As an example of what can be done, Rodney Brown, an accomplished mediator in his own right, described the work he has been doing at Uniondale High and other schools on Long Island.

Said Rodney, "During February, we took 30 your people up to Warrick for a conflict resolution retreat. Many people said it could not be done bringing together kids from Roosevelt, Uniondale and Hampstead - three rival, but connected communities. But we gave them four days of training, and it went beautifully."

Rodney said that the Warrick retreat was an outgrowth of training he and his associates had be conducting at Uniondale High School since early 1992. A group of 17 students have been highly successful in mediation disputes among their peers.

He said, "We have almost eliminated the violent response in Uniondale. There has not been a single fight over the winter. Some kids are now even saying they will boycott fights."

Said Rodney, "Kids do not listen to us, adults. You need a group of tenth graders to get to tenth graders. Young people have legitimate concerns, although they sometimes express them in inappropriate ways. Kids to listen to each other. Our peer leaders are saying to the others, "You can't talk to those grown folks -- come talk to us!"

He said, "We have had a program at Uniondale for two years. We have shown that 90% of these youth can become resolvers."

Rodney said that most of our kids really do not want to fight, but that they do it to prove themselves to their peers. This is the reason so many fights occur on school grounds. Kids who get along fine on the streets turn into violent adversaries at school. Rodney says that kids know there is always someone at the school who will break up the fight up before one of the combatants is seriously injured. It is the safest place to let everyone know that you will fight.

Conflict resolvers provide a means of "saving face" at the school without this resort to violence. Says Rodney, "At 16 American kids have seen over 200,000 acts of violence on television. They are shocked when people are really maimed or killed by the violence. On television, if somebody shoots somebody, they get up and appear on another channel. These kids want us to show them a "face-saving' alternative to the violence. We have shown them that way."

TO INCLUDE CONFLICT RESOLUTION IN PUBLIC SCHOOLS CURRICULUMS

All three of the Browns strongly advocate including the techniques of conflict resolution in the school's curricula, from as early age as possible.

Said Rodney, "Even elementary school students can be trained to be mediators, and it is important that we do it.'

Said Hezekiah, "Our schools are being turned out because of our social ills. Conflict resolution needs to be taught and called what it is. Otherwise, our schools will fall apart. We need to make it part of the curriculum."

HEZEKIAH BROWN
COLLECTION OF MEMORIES

HEZEKIAH BROWN
AWARDS AND RECOGNITIONS

Hez & Chris Brown receive Community Service Award

Hez Brown receive Man of Excellence Award

Hez Brown & Assoc receive Recognition from Councilwoman Dorothy Goosby

Honored by the Black Bar Association of Suffolk County

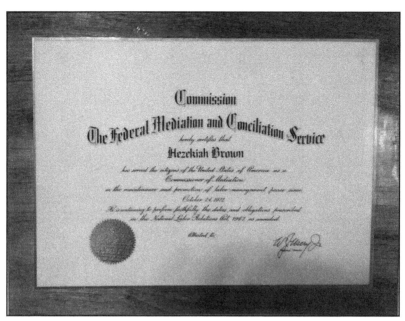

Federal Mediation & Conciliation Service Commission

President Ronald Regan awards Hez Brown
the Nation Community Service Award

The Presidential Inaugural Committee

requests the honor of your presence

to participate in the

inauguration of

Barack H. Obama

as President of the United States of America

and

Joseph R. Biden, Jr.

as Vice President of the United States of America

on Monday, the twenty-first of January

two thousand and thirteen

in the city of Washington

*Hez Brown attending Inauguration of the President and
Vice President opf the United States of America*

Governor Mario Cuomo endorses Hez Brown for Mayor of Hempstead

Hez Brown with Governor Roy Cooper

Hez Brown with Governor Jim Florio

Hez Brown with Governor Terry McAuliffe

The Brown Family

Hezekiah Brown in mediation service office in 1977.

Federal Mediator

Hezekiah Brown with Vice President Al Gore

Hezekiah Brown holds Press Conference announcing his plan to run for Mayor of Hempstead, New York

Hezekiah Brown with Supreme Court Judge Gerald Carter and Hempstead Village Justice Cynthia Diaz

Hezekiah Brown with Congresswoman Carolyn McCarthy and Bishop Frank White

Hezekiah Brown Teaching Conflict

Hezekiah Brown with Mayor David Dinkins
The First African-American to serve as Mayor of New York City

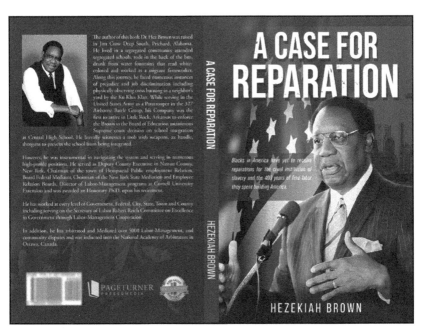

Hezekiah Brown A Case for Reparation Book

Hezekiah Brown Book Signing

COMMUNITY JOURNAL MAY 3

Brown wins Witherspoon-Harris Award

Community Relations panel
honors mediator, arbiter

By JULIAN EURE
Managing Editor

This year's recipient of the award named for two community leaders who worked to bridge conflict and promote unity is someone with a long record of doing similar work.

Dr. Hezekiah Brown, an expert in mediation, arbitration and conflict resolution, was awarded the 2018 Witherspoon-Harris Award by the Elizabeth City-Pasquotank Community Relations Commission during the panel's annual banquet at the K.E. White Center on Saturday.

Dr. Hirendranath Banerjee, chairman of the Community Relations Commission, said in an interview prior to Saturday's banquet that Brown was the commission's unanimous choice for this year's Witherspoon-Harris Award, after falling just a few votes short of winning it last year.

"He is somebody who came from a small Alabama town, who has

EROMY TILLMON/THE DAILY ADVANCE
Dr. Hirendranath Banerjee, (left) chairman of the Elizabeth City-Pasquotank Community Relations Commission, presents the commission's 2018 Witherspoon-Harris Award to Dr. Hezekiah Brown at the commission's annual banquet at the K.E. White Center, Saturday. About 30 people, including Mayor Bettie Parker, attended the event.

worked so hard for fair labor laws, and who has tried to bring communities together," Banerjee said. "He is an active member of this community. He is the ideal candidate for this award."

The award is named for two community leaders, neither of whom is still living: Cader Harris, a white businessman, and W.C. Witherspoon, a black educator and county commissioner. In the early 1990s, Harris and Witherspoon formed the Hope Group, a panel of private citizens still active in bridging racial and other divides in Elizabeth City through dialogue and face-to-face engagement.

Following up on the Hope Group's work, Elizabeth City City Council and the Pasquotank Board of Commissioners agreed to form the Community Relations Commission about a decade later. Under its rules, half the board's 16 members

are appointed by county commissioners, the other half by city councilors.

To honor Harris and Witherspoon's legacy, the Community Relations Commission began presenting an annual award named for them to persons who, according to Banerjee, provide "outstanding service to the community." Past honorees have included Gus Smith, Andy Montero, and just last year, Julie Robinson.

Reached prior to Saturday's banquet, Brown — himself a former longtime member of the Community Relations Commission — said receiving the award named for Witherspoon and Harris was a high honor.

"It means a tremendous amount to me," he said. "They saw something (injurious and hurtful) in the community coming and got ahead of it. They said, 'There's some probability of this happening and we should do something to prevent it.' They were proactive."

Although he never met Harris, Brown said he did

See BROWN, A5

Leaders must solve problems or be replaced

As I evaluate the status of our country and world events regarding basic human rights, relationships, and problem-solving, I conclude that we are in both an internal and external quandary that can only lead to more unnecessary conflict and violence. The unfortunate part is most individuals involved have not taken time to identify or evaluate the issues that continue to lead us down the path of separation and destruction.

I ask, what happened to the compassionate conservative? Where are the insightful liberals? Whatever happened to the ideals and principles upon which our country was founded, that justice shall prevail and all men are created equal? Respect, forgiveness, responsibility, love thy neighbor, do unto other as you would have them do unto you, when my brother hurts, I hurt; these principles seem to have been declared obsolete.

Instead, we are divided by political affiliation, race, trade wars, sanctions, threats of war, foreign policy, voter suppression, north, south, east, west, blue states, red states, religion, age, gender, wealth, poverty, abortion, guns, violence, bullying, same-sex marriages, health care, the minimum wage, infrastructure, immigration, the environment, climate change, and education.

The failure of our representatives to successfully address these important issues in a humanistic manner has created an environment of hate, fear and animosity which has spread through a large part of the country. In addition, this universal hostile environment has generated an increase in Neo-Nazi, Klux Klan and other hate groups. In fact, the Southern Poverty Law Center reported that the number of hate groups operating across America rose to a record high of 1,020 in 2018. It was the fourth straight year of hate group growth.

Racism and anti-Semitic violence continue to plague the country following the same escalation path as that of hate groups. In addition, there also has been an increase in physical violence in places like churches, schools, workplaces and nightclubs. It is apparent to me that too many of our elected representatives have given up on solving problems and resorted to

GUEST COLUMNIST

HEZEKIAH BROWN

street fighting, character assassination, and name calling. They only attempt to solve problems through crisis management and one-upmanship. The small number of attempts at negotiation that take place are influenced by derogatory name-calling and embarrassing personal attacks and end in failure. It is no longer about the people, or the problem, it's about the next election and who can win the finger-pointing blame game.

I have outlined why we have reached a point of near anarchy where problems are not being resolved by elected representatives at the highest levels of our federal, state, and some local governments. I contend their failure is why our country is so badly factionalized. We now have a generation of children adversely affected by violence and discord. Each day brings us another atrocity and still there appears to be little or no attempt by our leaders to reconcile differences. Therefore, it is time for the general public to make a statement. Our representatives must learn to problem-solve or be replaced.

I believe that they must learn six basic principles. Basically, they are: introspection, respect, understanding, empathy, acceptance and flexibility.

Things won't always be peaceful, nor will every resolution come peacefully. However, when we accept that conflict will happen, we can also accept that we will do our part to manage the conflict with as much respect as possible.

Successful problem-solving involves mutual gains, not winners and losers. If our elected representatives commit themselves to the above principles, we can create an environment in which our children and their children can grow and prosper without fear and hostility.

Hezekiah Brown is a resident of Elizabeth City.

The new Golden Rule favors those with gold

I have observed American politics for good part of my life, but never have I experienced the unashamed, wholesale attack on the working, middle and poor classes that is taking place under the Trump presidency.

More than ever I am reminded that there are two "Golden Rules." Most of us are familiar with the first "do unto others, etc." However, it appears the one followed by the Trump administration is "those who have the gold make the rules." And they make them for their own benefit. This is not new but one would be hard-pressed find anywhere in American history a more blatant transfer of wealth to the top 1 percent.

Make no mistake, the recent tax cut bill supported and signed by President Trump is one of the most devastating pieces of legislation ever perpetrated on American taxpayers. It is clearly a "Robin Hood in reverse" piece of legislation, taking from the poor to give to the rich. The multimillionaires and billionaires in the top 10 percent now have a huge permanent tax reduction. The other 90 percent of us will see our few dollars of tax benefit expire in a few short years. Then we or our children will have to pick up the cost.

But Trump insists that this was a great deal for working- and middle-class Americans. Trump even went so far as to claim this was "not a plan for the rich," that he personally wouldn't benefit from the legislation. There is no other way to say it: He flat out lied. It is been credibly estimated that he and his family will save approximately $25 million per year and as much as $1 billion over his lifetime. He who has the gold makes the rules.

This philosophy of robbing the poor to benefit the rich is further demonstrated through reducing regulations that protect all Americans. President Trump signed an executive order requiring agencies to repeal two regulations for every new regulation they adopt. He brags that this initiative has exceeded his expectations with 67 regulations rescinded so far and just three adopted a ratio of 22 to 1. He further boasts that repealing those old regulations has saved $8.1 billion in regulatory costs for big business.

GUEST COLUMNIST

HEZEKIAH BROWN

Trump appointed Scott Pruitt to head the Environmental Protection Agency. The mandate of the EPA is to protect human health and enforce environmental regulations. Yet since he was confirmed last February, Pruitt has worked to stall or roll back this core function of his agency. He has rolled back regulations on carbon emissions, clean water, and the use of chemicals. He has significantly reduced the agency's manpower thereby limiting the amount of staff inspections available to check pollutants and food, water, animal feed and chemicals used in agriculture. Trump's dismantling of the EPA puts every American at risk. It's not necessary to swim in clean water, but we certainly need to drink clean water. We need to breathe clean air. We need to eat uncontaminated meat and vegetables.

As if the wealthy hadn't prospered enough under the tax reform bill and deregulation, the recent "budget deal" dedicated billions more dollars to the top 1 percent. Yes, it included money for disaster relief, opioid addiction and veterans; extends the government's health insurance program for lower-income children; and increases domestic spending that Trump called a "waste."

Trump said it was a deal he had to make in order to get Democratic votes to take care of our military. But hidden in the folds of the budget deal are billions of dollars in tax breaks and bailouts for industry and business.

All across this country there are thousands of adults buying the wares of the greatest snake oil salesman ever elected president of these United States. It shows also they buy into he who has the gold makes the rules.

Hezekiah Brown is a retired former federal arbitrator and a resident of Elizabeth City.

How can region be the best? Collaboration

WE'RE NOT REALLY THE PARTY OF INFRASTRUCTURE...

I often state to residents, businesspeople and others that Elizabeth City-Pasquotank County is small and smart enough to serve as a role model for the rest of the nation.

How can this be, you ask?

First of all, we have tremendous resources in our county. We have some of the smartest and brightest individuals in the universe living and working right in our communities. Much of this talent goes unused because we have been too discreet about presenting a comprehensive and structured plan showing how they can contribute.

HEZEKIAH BROWN

I also believe that one of the major reasons we have not maximized use of our enormous amount of untapped skills and tremendous knowledge is that the opportunity was never as crystal clear as it is now.

As bad as this pandemic has been, it has taught us some lifetime lessons. And one of those lessons is: regardless of how much we have, where we work and where we live, and who we are, we need each other. There have been some heroic good deeds performed during this crisis. Neighbors have gotten to know each other; individuals have worked together to feed the hungry and lift up each other; families have spent time together. Many of the traditional things we take for granted have also changed. We worship differently. Kids go to school by Zoom. We funeralize our loved ones differently. We now work from home. The list goes on.

It's time, however, to work together to make Elizabeth City-

Pasquotank County the best of the best and we can do this by utilizing what we have right now: each other.

Just think, we have three outstanding institutions of higher learning right here: Elizabeth City State University, Mid-Atlantic Christian University and College of The Albemarle. ECSU has 2,002 students and approximately 627 full- and part-time employees; COA has 3,050 curriculum students and 185 full- and part-time faculty; and MACU has 139 students and 43 full- and part-time faculty and staff.

We also have the Elizabeth City-Pasquotank Public Schools, which has 4,954 students and 843 staff members. There is also the Northeast Academy for Aviation and Advanced Technologies, which has 750 students and approximately 65 full- and part-time faculty and staff members.

But we have more than schools. We have 850 personnel at the U.S. Coast Guard Base and 360 employees of the city of Elizabeth City. We also have Sentara Albemarle Medical Center, approximately 100 churches of all denominations, River City Community Development Corp., sororities, fraternities, Rotary Clubs, the Elizabeth City Area

Chamber of Commerce, Masons, a Lions Club, a 100 Black Men chapter, the National Association of University Women, the Chief Petty Officers Association, the Kiwanis Club, the American Association of Retired Persons, alumni associations, senior citizens associations, Veterans of Foreign Wars Post 6060, the Elizabeth City Networking Executives group, the Downtown Business & Professionals Association, and 2,569 businesses, including banks, Walmart, Lowe's and Hockmeyer Equipment Company.

We have the skills and knowledge right here to make, with just a little effort, our school district the best in the nation. We also can make our city and county the best in the nation. While we are currently involved in some collaborations and partnerships, just think what we could be if we really cooperated, collaborated, partnered and shared resources, skills and, in some instances, personnel. Think, for example, how much we could learn about information technology from the U.S. Coast Guard.

One of the areas where we fall far short is communication. We all know that Elizabeth City-Pasquotank County does

not have a television station to produce local news and promote the outstanding projects and amazing things we do in Elizabeth City. We depend solely on Virginia and Raleigh for our TV news. If we wanted to be creative, we could connect the city, county, and school district to teach students TV editing, production and on-air skills to prepare them for good-paying jobs in communications.

Pasquotank County is a Tier 1 county, which means it qualifies for extraordinary amounts of federal, state and other grants. However, it is my understanding the Elizabeth City-Pasquotank Public Schools does not have a full- or part-time grant writer. It seems we're leaving money on the table that could help bring in more grant funding to help the homeless, pay for innovative programs for the schools, and repair roads and complete other infrastructure projects.

This is a project that could be addressed by our three institutions of higher learning, the city, county and other community organizations. They could form a team that included grant writers from each organization. That team could then write applications seeking these grant funds for our communities.

In this community we have retired educators, scientists, engineers, military personnel, CEOs of large corporations, law enforcement personnel, information technology specialists, doctors, lawyers and skilled workers like mechanics, plumbers, electricians and carpenters. The list goes on.

Come on y'all. We can do this.

Hezekiah Brown is a resident of Elizabeth City.

Legislating fairness easy, legislating fair-mindedness isn't

In the past 50 years, the entire world has experienced an enormous amount of positive change through medical and advanced technology that has been beneficial to individuals, private industry and the U.S. government.

However, segments of the world that have not kept pace with this exceptional positive change in human relations, compassion and the attitudes and practices of people. Individuals and groups are still struggling when it comes to accepting change in how we treat each other.

Many of us are benefiting from the changes in medical and advanced technology, but failing when it comes to accepting the fact that it is only one race — the human race. We continue to be separated by the "haves" and "have not's," race, culture, religious beliefs and organizations.

Many individuals believe that we no longer are engaged in discrimination, prejudice, oppression and suppression because an African American was twice elected to the presidency. That kind of thinking is an antiquated and vastly exaggerated because

COLUMNIST

this president has faced more adversity than any other president in the history of our country. In fact, he and the first lady were caricatured as chimpanzees on social media.

Also, in the history of our country, no other president has had as many appointments filibustered as this president. Of all of the other 43 presidents, only 86 appointments were filibustered. Under Obama, 82 appointments have been filibustered in five years.

Furthermore, we cannot forget the fact that on the day of President Obama's first inauguration, a large number of highly elected officials had a meeting and made a pledge that they would not cooperate with this president, claiming "nothing would be accomplished under his presidency." They went on to say he would be a "one-term president."

Others have said they hope that he

HEZEKIAH BROWN

fails.

Some suggest that part of the problem is trust. Only a third of the public now says they have trust in their fellow Americans, according to one study. About half felt that way in 1972 when the general survey was done. Some blame this on the polarized politicians: Democrats against the Republicans, conservatives against the liberals, the independents and tea party against all of the above.

One of the things I have noticed over the past 50 years is that the U.S. Congress has tried to legislate fairness through civil rights legislation. They have passed anti-discrimination laws addressing housing, employment, civil rights and equal rights. The intention behind this legislation is positive. However, evidence shows that it is extremely difficult to legislate how individuals deal with someone they have been taught to dislike, as demonstrated by the

treatment of our president.

Children are not born prejudiced or disliking others who are different. They are taught through tradition, culture, and so-called family values to dislike others who are different, and this prejudicial thinking is passed on similar to "rites of passage" from generation to generation.

One of the most significant issues missed by the good-faith legislation is the humanistic part. Passing legislation without a component that brings people together has proven that individuals will do what they have to do until the next election where the positive legislation is challenged and watered down and ultimately becomes insignificant.

Christmas is the season where people truly demonstrate how we should treat others all year — with courtesy, love, respect, consideration, generosity. If that kind of good will could continue throughout the year, what a wonderful world this would be.

Hezekiah Brown is a certified mediator and lives in Elizabeth City.

Serving Elizabeth City and the Albemarle since 1911

The Daily Advance
Michael Goodman, *Publisher/Executive Editor*
Julian Eure, *Managing Editor*
Bob Montgomery, *News Editor*
A publication of Cooke Communications North Carolina, LLC

OPINIONS

More things change in politics, more they stay the same

After reflecting on the 2014 midterm election and engaging in conversation with some of my colleagues, many appeared to be shocked that Republicans were victorious in gaining seats in the U.S. Senate, Congress, state governor mansions and state legislatures.

In North Carolina, Republicans gained one seat in the state Senate for a 34-16 majority over the Democrats. Democrats gained three seats in the House where the Republicans hold a 74-46 majority. Republicans also hold 10 of 13 congressional seats in the state. The governor is also a Republican, although he wasn't on the ballot this November.

That means the Republicans are clearly in charge of the agenda for North Carolina. The question before the general public is how should we interpret this major victory? Does it mean that government will run smoother and more efficiently and be responsive to the masses? I can assure you that it will not, because power has a tendency to be misinterpreted and abused by those who possess it, whether they be Republicans or Democrats.

In fact, we have seen this movie numerous times before. Victory in national and local elections give the ruling party a false sense of power, which they say translates into a so-called mandate from the masses. That power and mandates generally last until the next election because the party that wins inevitably starts to misinterpret and misuse its perceived power and its so-called mandates. Invariably, they somehow forget about those who voted for the opposing party which includes Democrats, independents, unaffiliated voters and even those who exercise their right not to vote. In some instances, they attempt to discredit the politicians they replaced in the election, seriously believing, as the saying goes, that "to the victors belong the spoils" and punishing the loyal opposition. Unfortunately, our politicians are unable to take advantage of the history of elections and

COLUMNIST

HEZEKIAH BROWN

work to avoid falling victim to the past.

In fact, history shows that the president's party (whether it be Republican or Democrat) almost always get shellacked in midterm elections. Only twice — in 1834 and 2002 — did the president's party actually gain seats in both the House and Senate.

President Bill Clinton, who was first elected in 1992, struggled with the conservative faction in both the Republican and Democratic parties which handed Republicans their greatest victory in the mid-term election two years later. Republicans picked up 54 seats in the House of Representatives and gained eight seats in the Senate, while also taking control of a number of governorships and state legislatures.

In 2006, it was easy to blame everything on President Bush because the Republicans controlled both the House and the Senate. As a result primarily of the Iraq war, the 2006 midterm election resulted in a sweeping victory for Democrats, who captured control of the House and Senate, while also winning a majority of governorships and control of state legislatures.

In 2014, we witnessed a repeat of the essence of midterm elections where the Republicans captured both House and Senate and won a large number of governorships and control of state legislatures.

So as I stated earlier, we have seen this movie before. So was it really President Barack Obama or was it the ghost of midterm elections that influenced approximately 60 percent of the voting public to stay home and not participate in the elections? The final question is: did they refuse to vote because they had lost confidence in our system of governing?

In my opinion, this movie will continue to play as long as the elected officials continue this "get me today and I'll get you tomorrow" blame game instead of governing for the people.

Hezekiah Brown is a resident of Elizabeth City

Rebuilding America requires rebuilding people

The $1 trillion infrastructure bill President Biden signed into law in November 2021 was a long time coming and will be great for many Americans. It will rebuild roads, airports, railroads and bridges, replacing degenerated plumbing. It will also create good-paying jobs.

It is essential and extremely vital to rebuild and replace our failing infrastructure. But we have another huge and pervasive problem that also needs fixing: our failing human infrastructure. While the brick-and-mortar rebuilding of America is of utmost importance, it is equally important to build people.

We witness on a daily basis how anger, hatred, systemic racism and mental illness are eroding and destroying the human infrastructure of our country. The failure of our elected officials to address these issues is fundamentally irresponsible and borders on contempt.

Unfortunately, we cannot rely on our elected officials in Washington, D.C. to solve these problems because many of our elected officials' only concern is their next

HEZEKIAH BROWN

election. Still others have purposefully turned a blind eye to the eroding American promise.

American politicians have spent trillions of taxpayer dollars protecting other countries, justifying the expense by claiming they are "killing their own people." I do not understand why these politicians refuse to see that Americans are killing other Americans at an extremely high rate without any solutions. We are experiencing an inordinate amount of violence across the country, including mass killings, drive-by shootings, homicides, suicides and killings by law enforcement.

As we read this, more than 9,800 people have lost their lives this year due to gun violence. As of this date, there have been approximately 129 mass shootings, with no end in sight.

We seem to be taking care of the problem by buying more guns and ammunition

for ourselves — either to get ready for a civil war or to protect our families. What a tragedy! There are more privately owned guns in the good old USA than people. We know of at least 398 million guns as of May of last year, and that's not counting those that are not reported.

In addition, hate groups are at an all-time high. According to the Southern Poverty Law Center, North Carolina had 28 hate groups in 2021 that spew hatred. Among them are neo-Nazis, Black and White nationalists, and groups whose members are anti-Muslim, anti-immigrant and anti-LGBTQ. Others are Holocaust deniers, White nationalists and Black nationalists.

While these hate groups are running rampant and continuing to grow and create chaos, we have many Americans — Black, White and others — who understand the importance of diversity and equal rights. We, the majority of Americans, must start speaking up for what is right for all people. Our political leadership has failed miserably in dealing with systematic racism

and people of color. Race relations are widening, and individuals are drawing lines in the sand — with Whites on one side and Blacks on the other.

We must demand that our political leaders commit to an open and pluralistic society and put in place systems and methods to rebuild our human infrastructure. We need resources and methodologies to teach tolerance, reason and empathy.

Sure, we need to continue to rebuild our infrastructure: America still needs new bridges, roads, airports, railroads, waterways and sewer systems.

However, if we continue to ignore our human infrastructure needs — how we deal with racism, eliminate discrimination and intolerance, and treat each other — rebuilding our brick-and-mortar infrastructure will not matter. All the shiny new asphalt is still meaningless if we do not build bridges between people.

Dr. Hezekiah Brown is a resident of Camden, Delaware, and a former resident of Elizabeth City.

Our schools should teach conflict resolution

We live in a world full of conflict, anger and frustration, and this ultimately leads to physical and psychological violence resulting in today's terrible crime and war statistics.

This world is especially dangerous for our youth who are ill-equipped to control their anger because they are, by and large, not taught how to resolve conflict in their household, school or community.

HEZEKIAH BROWN

In addition, they observe violence daily through games, television, sports, politics and in the community. We are aggrieved by the statistics on infant mortality, child abuse, violence in our schools, teenage crime, and gang violence but fail to seriously address this issue.

We fear that our society seems locked in a cycle, as children are born into violent circumstances, grow up in fear, and finally themselves become violent people — starting the cycle all over again. In my opinion, the only way to break this cycle is to start teaching our children how to resolve conflict instead of resorting to violence. We need to make conflict resolution and anger management a mandatory part of the school curriculum.

Because individuals interact with other individuals, there is always the potential for conflict. Conflict is inevitable when people's attitudes, values, goals and expectations differ. But most conflict can be resolved without resorting to violence.

Frankly, it is not the conflict itself, but how the parties go about trying to resolve conflict that, in may instances, creates problems. The manner in which you approach the conflict will determine whether you reach a positive outcome or continue the conflict. Conflicts are an inevitable part of living in a society, but conflict can be resolved without violence.

We all understand that devastation results from the use of violence. We further understand that violence destroys and that violence begets violence. Yet, we allow ourselves to be seduced by violence. We study violence, we cultivate violence, and in the heat of conflict, we readily resort to violence, accomplishing harm which we often regret for the rest of our lives. We say hurtful things we sometimes wish we could take back to those we love in order to hurt them.

To gain possession of a skill, one must first understand what the skill is, what one can do with it, and how that skill operates. However, one must then devote the necessary time and teaching to master that skill. One must study, and practice, practice, practice what one learns. Being taught a skill saves years of trial and error. Simply learning to perform self-examination, exchanging positions with the other party and developing good listening skills, are the initial steps to learning how to resolve conflict.

In addition, learning to apologize when you know that you have offended someone, showing compassion, and practicing forgiveness are essential conflict-resolution skills.

Learning to resolve conflicts is tantamount to learning to swim or ride a bicycle. Once you learn it, you never forget. Therefore, I believe that it is essential that we examine the feasibility of implementing conflict resolution as part of our local school curriculum. It will pay tremendous dividends.

Hezekiah Brown is a resident of Elizabeth City. He is a retired federal mediator.

SOMETHING TO SAY

Send your letters to:
Letters to the Editor, P.O. Box 588, Elizabeth City, NC 27907-0588
Email elizabethcity@dailyadvance.com
Fax (252) 335-4143

Please limit letters to 300 words and include your name, address, phone number and email address (if applicable). We use phone and address to contact writers, but do not publish that information.

Questions about a letter?
Call Julian Eure, managing editor, at (252) 329-9680 or email jeure@dailyadvance.com
Read more from us and our contributors at dailyadvance.com/opinion.

4A THE DAILY ADVANCE, FRIDAY, OCTOBER 23, 2015

Serving Elizabeth City and the Albemarle since 1911

The Daily Advance
Michael Goodman, *Publisher/Executive Editor*
Julian Eure, *Managing Editor*
Bob Montgomery, *News Editor*
A publication of Cooke Communications North Carolina, LLC

OPINIONS

Entire community must come to aid of at-risk students

Several weeks ago, I read an article in The Daily Advance regarding a report made by Dr. Larry Cartner, superintendent of the Elizabeth City-Pasquotank Public Schools, to the Pasquotank County Chapter of the NAACP which shared valuable information pertaining to our African-American students.

Cartner said that black students' achievement rates lagged between 11 and 40 percentage points behind those for their white peers. Alarmingly, he also stated that black students represented 60 percent of all students who were not promoted to the next grade last year. He appealed to the local NAACP chapter for help in getting African-American students to attend their classes. He stressed that of the 231 students held back a grade in 2014-15, 139 were black. Black males are being suspended at twice the rate of white males, he said.

After initially reading the article, I was devastated and angry. I also was disappointed after learning that third-grade students had an extremely high rate of absenteeism, and there was such a high disparity among students along racial lines. If third-graders are not attending class, regardless of the reasons, they are being set up for failure due to the long-term impact it will have on them, their families and society.

We must be reminded that recent research has shown that correctional institutions are built in various communities based on the evaluation of third-grade students. If students are performing poorly in the 3rd grade, state agencies are encouraged to build more prisons in those areas at an astronomical cost to the taxpayers. So we should address the problem now or pay for it later. In addition, if our children are not performing at least at grade level, they become candidates for

GUEST COLUMNIST

HEZEKIAH BROWN

the "school-to-prison" cycle.

Moreover, I concluded that if third-graders are not attending classes, it's not their fault. It is the fault of their guardian, which really perpetuates the issue and makes it more devastating and poses more serious consequences for the children.

After evaluating and digesting the entire report made by the superintendent, I began to ask the question, what can I and other community members do to assist in this abnormal situation to curtail this vicious cycle? Keep in mind, there are certain obstacles that must be taken into consideration.

For example, the numerous single parents (a lot of them teenagers) who are unequipped to deal with the various problems they face on a daily basis trying to raise children alone. In other instances, grandparents and foster parents who are caring for some of these children are also ill-equipped to deal with difficult children.

Therefore, we must build a strong community support system and join with the superintendent, teachers and administrators in addressing this serious epidemic we are facing. The only ones who can save us, is us.

In fact, I noted that there are in excess of 100 churches in Pasquotank County, numerous fraternities, sororities, professional organizations, businesses and colleges and universities. There are also ECSU alumni, retiree associations, high school alumni, Veterans of Foreign War posts, veterans associations, the AARP, Masons and social clubs. The list goes on and on.

In my opinion, it is time for our community members to signd up for children by volunteering a small portion of their time to this school district in support of our children.

Hezekiah Brown is a resident of Elizabeth City.

Serving Elizabeth City and the Albemarle since 1911

The Daily Advance
Michael Goodman, *Publisher/Executive Editor*
Julian Eure, *Managing Editor*
A publication of Cooke Communications North Carolina, LLC

OPINIONS

Start caring about youth before they give up hope on life

GUEST COLUMNIST

HEZEKIAH BROWN

Several years ago I was asked to speak to a group of African-American youth about turning their lives around and becoming good, law-abiding citizens. I stressed the importance of education, employment, self-esteem, fatherhood and family values. Incidentally, many of the youth in this group had been labeled incorrigible and some had been in the criminal justice system for years.

As I started talking to this group, I noticed a sense of insecurity and a lack of interest. I could see that I was not getting across to these young men. I then changed my approach and started to question them about their future, family, fatherhood and their long-term interests. Those questions created the beginning of a long and serious dialogue. Incidentally, a large number of the youth lived in single-family homes, some lived in shelters and other did not have a place called home.

As the dialogue advanced, these young men informed me they were doomed for life because they had committed felonies and would be ineligible to get a good-paying job. Even after serving their time they are still being punished for the same crime. In fact, one of these young men referred to a felony sentence as a life sentence that forced individuals into a lifetime of second-class citizenship. They expressed to me that they were not going to subscribe to second-class citizenship under any circumstances. They were pretty adamant

about their positions and showed no signs or caring about the long-term consequences or valuing life as most of us know it.

Many of these young men stated that they knew that they were going to die before they reached the age of 25, so be it. If they completed their education, it would not change their status or contribute to them getting a good-paying job because of their label as a felon. Therefore, in their opinion, they felt they were relegated to a life of gangs, drug dealing, burglary and other forms of crime due to the standards set by society.

I shared my work experience and the importance of being a good, law-abiding citizen with this group of young men. I further stressed the pitfalls and detriment of becoming a professional criminal who gets caught up in our criminal injustice system.

A large number of individuals are incarcerated for low level crimes and truly receive a life sentence once a felony is committed. Many believe that in order to solve these problems, the solution should be to build more jails and lock up these individuals. Obviously, that kind of thinking is not working because those who are incarcerated serve time and return back to society without any skills, and, in too many instances, they resort to crime in order to survive.

As many know, we are dealing with a serious phenomenon without any long-term solutions. It is my belief that if we are going to solve a problem, we must first define the problem. We then must seek rational, reasonable and doable solutions to address the specific problem. If we define the wrong problem, we will certainly create the wrong solution.

The fact is, many of those individuals who have given up on life and are not afraid of dying, or killing others or going to jail is a problem that needs to be addressed. In my opinion, we recently witnessed some of those youngsters when approximately 50 individuals were killed in Chicago. In Baltimore, 40 individuals were killed in one month. I believe that many of those involved in these shootings fit the profile of that group of young men I met with who had given up on life. When one gives up on their own life, they do not value the lives of others.

We must address the issue of lifetime sentencing that prohibits some individuals who could be rehabilitated and becoming model citizens if given the right opportunity. In addition, we must encourage correctional institutions to offer survival and life skills that individuals can use as they return to society. We must re-educate those

individuals by offering vocational programs while they are incarcerated so they will have the skills to survive when they're released. In most instances, if individuals have the vocational skills to become painters, plumbers, electricians, landscapers, brick masons, carpenters, auto mechanics, computer repairmen or chefs, they have the opportunity to fill a void instead of seeking employment where they would be rejected due to their criminal background.

I firmly believe that we must use a multitude of approaches and strategies, including engaging the entire community and stakeholders in solving this problem. Moreover, the issues that we face simply cannot wait until the next young person is killed and the individual who killed him is arrested, and we dust off all our protest boots and march for justice. We must join together and create a dialogue with all parties that could potentially be affected. We must start to address the issues at hand and collectively seek reasonable approaches to these systemic problems.

In addition, those communities that are not facing the same kind of issues regarding violence must be pro-active and start to address these issues before the crises arrive. We must create credible programs that can be replicated in other areas that will give some of those who have given up on life a better vision and assure them that we care.

Hezekiah Brown is a resident of Elizabeth City

Not controlling anger unhealthy for us, society

HEZEKIAH BROWN

Anger is one of the most difficult, unforeseen and emotional issues that we have to learn to deal with. In fact, anger essentially affects every organ in the body. It simultaneously affects your heart, blood pressure, nervous system, vision, hearing and other organs, and can cause more harm to the individual who is angry than to the person with whom they are angry.

Individuals who are unable to control their anger have suffered heart attacks or strokes, and have even died due to their inability to control their anger. Therefore it is incumbent upon all individuals to understand the detriment uncontrollable anger can cause.

Anger is an emotion that can range from mild irritation to intense rage. While many people categorize anger as solely "negative emotions," it can also be positive. Angry feelings, for example, may spur you to stand up for someone or lead you to

create social change.

However, left unchecked, angry feelings can also lead to aggressive physical behavior, including yelling at someone or damaging their property. Angry feelings also may cause you to withdraw from the world and turn your anger inward, which can affect your health and well-being.

Anger becomes problematic when it's felt too often or too intensely or when it's expressed in unhealthy ways. This can take a toll on us physically, mentally and socially. For this reason, anger management strategies can be beneficial and can help one discover healthy ways to express one's feelings.

I have taught classes on managing anger. In teaching the

class, one of the questions we ask individuals is: What do you do when you get angry?

Many of those answering the question admit to "losing it" when they get angry. Others simply say that they don't really remember what they did when they became angry. This anger is the root cause of the physical violence that can lead to someone losing their life.

I recall going to Rikers Island, a correctional institution in the East River in New York City, to conduct a training program for inmates on managing conflict and anger. At the conclusion of the program, one of the inmates who was serving a life sentence thanked me for sharing information on how to resolve conflict.

He further stated that he truly enjoyed the program and that if he and some of his fellow inmates had received some training on managing conflict and anger, some of them probably would not be

incarcerated. He further stated that an individual "dissed him" and, because he could not control his anger, he killed that person. In that instance, two individuals lost their lives: the individual who was killed and the individual who committed the crime.

There are thousands and thousands of instances of this kind of violence. Our society believes that the solution is to "lock up" those who commit violence instead of being pro-active and instituting conflict resolution and anger management teaching/training programs in our schools, churches and community organizations.

I believe that individuals who learn to resolve conflict and manage their anger will have a tool that almost guarantees success in their relationships, work environment, family and community.

Hezekiah Brown is a resident of Elizabeth City.

Serving Elizabeth City and the Albemarle since 1911

The Daily Advance
Michael Goodman, *Publisher/Executive Editor*
Julian Eure, *Managing Editor*
A publication of Cooke Communications North Carolina, LLC

OPINIONS

Conflict resolution in classrooms could curb violence

The United States of America is the most advanced and powerful nation in the world when it comes to military preparedness, advanced technology, economics and standard of living. With a few exceptions, we are holding our own and can compete globally in every area.

One area where we fall far short and lack any strategic plans for improvement is in our response to physical and psychological violence. We are fundamentally unable to grasp the essence and root causes of violence, and this prohibits us from seeking the appropriate solutions when dealing with violence and race relations.

Physical violence such as assault, rape or murder is an extreme form of aggression. It's behavior in which physical force is exerted for the purpose of causing damage or injury. Psychological violence is anything that an individual or group does to knowingly harm others, be it verbally, mentally, morally, racially, criminally, sexually or emotionally. Psychological violence is by and large rendered with the tongue; timing and tone can be as devastating as physical violence. The strongest person physically can be adversely injured by words.

In fact, gun violence is one of the most deadly components of violence. Approximately 90 individuals are gunned down through gun violence daily. Meanwhile, segregation and discrimination are rampant and appear to be acceptable as a way of life. We have the haves against the have nots, whites against blacks, blacks against whites, rich against poor, males against females, religion against religion, young against old. All of these conflicts are a form of violence.

Obviously, there is a reason for our failure in these areas. In my opinion, the basic reason for our failures and our reluctance to address these complex issues is, simply put, economics. Address this phenomena is going to cost money, and most institutions are unwilling to make the investment.

In fact, our country is home to some of the most prestigious colleges and universities, each doing an excellent job preparing students for the world of work. However, we fail miserably when it comes to teaching our children how to manage conflict and deal with diversity. We fail to formally teach our children and advanced students how to manage and solve problems beyond the academic ones they encounter in the classroom.

GUEST COLUMNIST

HEZEKIAH BROWN

room. Managing conflict is a skill that can be taught to children and adults. Learning to solve conflict is like learning to swim or ride a bicycle. Once learned, you never forget it. Just think, children are not born violent. Violence is a learned behavior and children by and large become a product of their environment. Children are not born hating others who don't look or worship like them. This hatred is taught to them as they grow up, and is passed along from generation to generation – similar to a rite of passage – by their elders for no rational reason other than meanness.

This behavior has now spilled over into all segments of our society, even politics, where it is now fashionable to stereotype individuals because of their religion, race, sex, sexual orientation or national origin. This happens without any consequences, compassion or feeling for those adversely affected by it.

In my opinion, one of the methods available to address the problem is within our reach. I believe that learning the humanistic approach to problem-solving at an early age is essential to our society's success and will ultimately save lives and money. Many of those who are incarcerated possibly could have avoided going to prison had they been taught some basic skills in resolving conflict. These skills could have been taught in our schools since most children are not taught problem-solving skills at home. Managing conflict and diversity should be a mandatory part of the school curriculum because it will better prepare our children for the real world. Children need to be taught the importance of self-examination, forgiveness, apology, compassion and developing good listening skills in order to become a holistic person.

Because of the size of the problem and the limitation on teachers and administrators in terms of discipline, there has to be a different approach. I believe that in order to address this critical problem, every school district should implement a mandatory conflict-resolution training program for grades K-12. I recognize that there are costs involved. I also realize that this recommendation is not the ultimate panacea. However, if implemented in our schools, a conflict-resolution training program would pay tremendous dividends, ultimately saving lives and money and, in some instances, preventing incarceration.

We can do better.

Hezekiah Brown is a resident of Elizabeth City

Serving Elizabeth City and the Albemarle for 99 years

The Daily Advance

OPINIONS

Addressing bullying, gang and gun violence

After reading a number of articles recently in local media regarding gangs, gun violence and bullying, I decided to respond and offer a few solutions on how to address a global issue that has a devastating impact on our schools and communities on a daily basis. In fact, there is hardly a single day that passes in which we do not hear of young children and adults being killed or wounded by gunfire. Just recently, it was reported that a 4-year-old child was attending church service and was hit by a stray bullet.

It is time for us as a community to take some action.

The United States is still the most powerful and sophisticated nation in the world. We have been successful in advanced technology, putting a man on the moon, placing satellites in space and leading the world in social development. Unfortunately, this has not trickled down to the young people in the minority communities in North Carolina and Virginia.

Somehow, these advances seem to escape the minority community, especially in our schools and communities. Violence, bullying and conflict have come to be a way of life in our schools. Our children seem to lack the social skills needed to handle and manage these issues.

COLUMNIST

HEZEKIAH BROWN

Let's take a look at bullying, for example, a pervasive issue in our schools. Recent statistics around bullying are frightening:

- 8 percent of students miss one day of school per month;
- 43 percent of students fear harassment in school bathrooms;
- 20 percent of the time, arguments with a bully result in physical altercations;
- 30 percent of students have heard another student threaten to kill someone;
- 20 percent of students know of other students who bring guns to school;
- Every 7 minutes a child is bullied, increasing violence on school grounds;
- 282,000 students are physically attacked in schools each month; and
- Most of the violence actually occurs on school grounds.

Analyzing this data produces frightening repercussions. Our children are facing the battle. They are on the frontline of American gang conflict. In fact, the death of a minority student is having a profound impact. Ironically, this life expectancy of an entire race of people. Violence is having a powerful impact on young people in North Carolina and Virginia.

Traditional methods of dealing with these issues have failed miserably. Suspension, expulsion and other traditional methods of discipline have no impact because they do not address the fundamental issues of values, attitudes and beliefs. We tell young people to "STOP IT," but we don't give them alternatives or replacements for managing anger commensurate, effectively and with positive, peaceful ways.

Violence is not an innate phenomenon, but a learned one as young people cope with the environment with the skills they have learned; fighting, strength, and disrespect. This is a sad testament to the adults that have dropped the ball.

To address these issues, we must develop a comprehensive and sustained approach to school violence. Students must learn appropriate methods of resolving conflict that will stay with them throughout their adult lives. I am proposing all community stakeholders invest in our youth by investing in their social skills.

Many urban areas across the country are addressing these issues through the utilization of conflict resolution programs in schools that include peer mediation, character development and peacemaker programs. These programs utilize the most influential resource we have to combat these issues: students.

These programs focus on the development of social skills that help young people cope with the issues they face. Some of these issues include:

- Listening
- Communication
- Negotiation
- Anger Management
- Character development
- Mediation.

The development of these comprehensive programs has proven to be effective in reducing violence, bullying, suspension and expulsions.

I believe that teaching young people the values associated with managing conflict, we can address other issues that may be lacking. We should teach children the values of compassion, forgiveness and the humility associated with the art of apologizing for behavior that negatively affects others.

Hezekiah Brown, an arbitrator and former federal mediator, is a resident of Elizabeth City

Managing anger is something we all can learn

A s I read the national and local news and watch television, I am amazed at the amount of anger and animosity being spewed through street fights, shootings, domestic violence and bar brawls. There are even some instances where government officials are actually fist fighting. These violent behaviors happen primarily because those engaging in them have not been introduced to the 4 R's: Respect, Rights, Responsibility and Restrictions. We must learn to deal with anger and animosity.

In learning to resolve conflict, it is essential that one learn to manage anger first. Of all of the human emotional feelings individuals experience daily, anger is the most powerful and poorly handled. Although anger is considered to be a healthy normal human emotion, it varies in intensity from mild irritation to intense fury and rage. It has the ability to take control and become destructive, leading to unforeseen problems in your work and personal life, jeopardizing your and others' quality of life.

Anger is a stronger feeling

HEZEKIAH BROWN

than love and can have a devastating impact on individuals who are unable to control their anger. In fact, anger affects the individual who is angry more than it affects the individual or individuals you are angry with.

For example, if you are angry at an individual every time you are in their presence, it affects you. Therefore, it is incumbent on you to seek methods to deal with your anger.

In addition, many are unable to understand the impact that anger has on the body. Anger affects every organ in your body. It also affects blood pressure, your hearing, vision, breathing and entire nervous system. Anger causes heart attacks and strokes.

In fact, of all the human emotional feelings, anger is the most powerful. Although anger is considered to be a healthy normal human emotion, it varies in intensity from mild irritation to

intense fury and rage. It has the ability to take control and become damaging and destructive.

Moreover, most individuals really cannot recall what they say or what happened when they get angry. When asked "what do you do when you get angry?" many respond truthfully. They said they curse, strike others or hit a wall, use alcohol, do drugs, take revenge, shut down, name call, speed drive, get violent, cry and in some cases wish the other party was dead.

All of the reactions to anger are by and large negative and harmful to the individual and others. It confirms that anger can be a friend or an enemy depending on how you choose to express it.

Responding aggressively is the natural way to express anger. It is a natural adaptive response to threats. Anger inspires powerful, often-aggressive feelings and behaviors that allow us to fight and defend ourselves when attacked. Therefore, one can say that anger is necessary for survival. Feelings of anger are normal, something experienced by everyone,

and a powerful feeling that one can learn to manage.

People use a variety of processes, both conscious and unconscious, to deal with their angry feelings. One cannot change, avoid or get rid of the things or people that enrage them. However, one can learn to control your reaction to anger. Knowing how to recognize and express it appropriately can help you reach your goals, solve problems, handle emergencies effectively, and protect your health.

The inability to recognize and understand one's anger can lead to a variety of personal difficulties. Not until you learn to change your attitudes will you have the power and freedom to be your own person, capable of determining and achieving your goals and dreams.

It is not easy to change negative attitudes. It takes time and practice. Being able to act instead of react, and see an opportunity instead of a problem, is the greatest gift you can give yourself. We can do better.

Hezekiah Brown is a resident of Elizabeth City.

4A THE DAILY ADVANCE, SATURDAY, APRIL 4, 2015

Serving Elizabeth City and the Albemarle since 1911

The Daily Advance
Michael Goodman, *Publisher/Executive Editor*
Julian Eure, *Managing Editor*
Bob Montgomery, *News Editor*
A publication of Cooke Communications North Carolina, LLC

OPINIONS

Forgiveness as important as apologizing for wrong

I believe the media did a few things right in the racial harmony front recently in its handling of two controversial matters that had far-reaching negative implications. It reported on two incidents in which individuals did something right by apologizing, asking for forgiveness and showing compassion for those who were possibly offended by their behavior.

In the first instance, it reported one of the students involved in a fraternity ceremony at Oklahoma State University. During the incident, a student was observed on camera chanting derogatory remarks about African Americans and using a racial slur. That individual admitted that he had erred in participating in the ceremony and was wrong for using the slur. On national television, he also apologized to the president of Oklahoma State University, its students, the community and the nation.

The second incident involved a baseball player at Bloomsburg University in Pennsylvania who happened to be white tweet-

ing a derogatory and degrading remark about Mo'ne Davis, the African-American female baseball player who participated in last year's Little League World Series. When Bloomsburg University learned of the incident, the player was suspended from the baseball team. Davis then went on television and said she had forgiven the player, and urged the president of Bloomsburg to reinstate him. Her rationale was that we all make mistakes and deserve a second chance. I believe she went on to say that she was not offended by the remarks.

In fact, if the truth is spoken, we all have made dreadful remarks that we wish we could take back. However, in most instances, we are so embarrassed and fail to realize how some spoken words affect others. We are unaware of how to correct what we've said. As a result, the hurt lin-

COLUMNIST

HEZEKIAH BROWN

gers on — in some instances for a lifetime — and long-standing friendships are lost.

What subsequently happened after these two painful incidents is by and large unprecedented. After it was revealed that these two individuals had committed these biased infractions, some swift actions were taken for which all involved should be commended.

In one instance, the individual apologized. In the other, the person who was the subject of the offense defended the action of the offender. One of the major problems in our world is the unwillingness of individuals to forgive. Another is an unwillingness to accept forgiveness. The same applies to apologizing. If one does something to offend another individual, it is not unmanly to apologize and doing so doesn't show weakness. In fact,

it shows character and strength. We have to learn the importance of forgiveness and teaching others to forgive and take action to show compassion for others.

The moral of this story is there is much to be learned from these two incidents, not the least of which were the swift actions taken by the two universities to suspend the baseball player and the fraternity whose members had made the offensive remarks, or that the universities plan to offer diversity training to students and staff. More important is the way the two young people at the center of the controversies have reacted. The young man at Oklahoma State University was contrite in acknowledging his mistake. He also expressed a willingness to speak out against racial injustices.

Perhaps even more important is the lesson of forgiveness shown by Mo'ne Davis. Imagine our environment if we all could learn to apologize and forgive.

Hezekiah Brown is a resident of Elizabeth City

Serving Elizabeth City and the Albemarle since 1911

The Daily Advance
Michael Goodman, *Publisher/Executive Editor*
Julian Eure, *Managing Editor*
A publication of Cooke Communications North Carolina, LLC

OPINIONS

Start caring about youth before they give up hope on life

Several years ago I was asked to speak to a group of African-American youth about turning their lives around and becoming good, law-abiding citizens. I stressed the importance of education, employment, self-esteem, fatherhood and family values. Incidentally, many of the youth in this group had been labeled incorrigible and some had been in the criminal justice system for years.

As I started talking to this group, I noticed a sense of insecurity and a lack of interest. I could see that I was not getting across to these young men. I then changed my approach and started to question them about their future, family, fatherhood and their long-term interests. Those questions created the beginning of a long and serious dialogue. Incidentally, a large number of the youth lived in single-family homes, some lived in shelters and other did not have a place called home.

As the dialogue advanced, these young men informed me they were doomed for life because they had committed felonies and would be ineligible to get a good-paying job. Even after serving their time they are still being punished for the same crime. In fact, one of these young men referred to a felony sentence as a life sentence that forced individuals into a lifetime of second-class citizenship. They expressed to me that they were not going to subscribe to second-class citizenship under any circumstances. They were pretty adamant

about their positions and showed no signs or caring about the long-term consequences or valuing life as most of us know it.

Many of these young men stated that they knew that they were going to die before they reached the age of 25, so be it. If they completed their education, it would not change their status or contribute to them getting a good-paying job because of their label as a felon. Therefore, in their opinion, they felt they were relegated to a life of gangs, drug dealing, burglary and other forms of crime due to the standards set by society.

I shared my work experience and the importance of being a good, law-abiding citizen with this group of young men. I further stressed the pitfalls and detriment of becoming a professional criminal who gets caught up in our criminal justice system.

A large number of individuals are incarcerated for low level crimes and truly receive a life sentence once a felony is committed. Many believe that in order to solve these problems, the solution should be to build more jails and lock up these individuals. Obviously, that kind of thinking is not working because those who are incarcerated serve time and return back to society without any skills and, in too many instances, they resort to crime in order to survive.

GUEST COLUMNIST

HEZEKIAH BROWN

As many know, we are dealing with a serious phenomenon without any long-term solutions. It is my belief that if we are going to solve a problem, we must first define the problem. We then must seek rational, reasonable and doable solutions to address the specific problem. If we define the wrong problem, we will certainly create the wrong solution.

The fact is, many of those individuals who have given up on life and are not afraid of dying, or killing others or going to jail is a problem that needs to be addressed. In my opinion, we recently witnessed some of those youngsters when approximately 50 individuals were killed in Chicago. In Baltimore, 40 individuals were killed in one month. I believe that many of those involved in these shootings fit the profile of that group of young men I met with who had given up on life. When one gives up on their own life, they do not value the lives of others.

We must address the issue of lifetime sentencing that prohibits some individuals who could be rehabilitated and becoming model citizens if given the right opportunity. In addition, we must encourage correctional institutions to offer survival and life skills that individuals can use as they return to society. We must re-educate those

individuals by offering vocational programs while they are incarcerated so they will have the skills to survive when they're released. In most instances, if individuals have the vocational skills to become painters, plumbers, electricians, landscapers, brick masons, carpenters, auto-mechanics, computer repairmen or chefs, they have the opportunity to fill a void instead of seeking employment where they would be rejected due to their criminal background.

I firmly believe that we must use a multitude of approaches and strategies, including engaging the entire community and stakeholders in solving this problem. Moreover, the issues that we face simply cannot wait until the next young person is killed and the individual who killed him is arrested, and we dust off our protest boots and march for justice. We must join together and create a dialogue with all parties that could potentially be affected. We must start to address the issues at hand and collectively seek reasonable approaches to these systemic problems.

In addition, those communities that are not facing the same kind of issues regarding violence must be pro-active and start to address these issues before the crises arrive. We must create credible programs that can be replicated in other areas that will give some of those who have given up on life a better vision and assure them that we care.

Hezekiah Brown is a resident of Elizabeth City

We can't afford to wait for gun violence 'vaccine'

Thankfully, we have found a way to end the terrible COVID-19 pandemic. Over half-a-million American lives have been lost to the disease. While our thoughts and prayers went out to their families, we did more. We developed vaccines in record time to combat the scourge.

Yet there is another deadly plague sweeping across our nation and it has been taking more and more lives every year: gun violence and mass shootings.

As you read this, more than 13,142 people have lost their lives so far this year due to gun violence. In 2021, the U.S. has averaged more than one mass shooting a day. As of this date there have been 157 mass shooting incidents across America, including five here in North Carolina.

Thoughts and prayers cannot fix this problem. We cannot wait until the scientists find the formula to address this phenomena. Passing more legislation might be part of the solution but it is not the panacea for fixing all of

HEZEKIAH BROWN

the issues involved because it is impossible to legislate emotions, anger, racial hatred and attitudes.

Building more jails and hiring more police officers or waiting for politicians to act is not going to solve the problem. This epidemic must be addressed through the humanistic approach. Individuals must be taught how to deal with anger and emotions. They must learn conflict-resolution skills. Nearly every area of life sometimes requires implementing effective conflict-resolution strategies.

There is an old adage "You can't teach an old dog new tricks." So for many adults how they learned conflict resolution in childhood is how they respond to conflict today. Typically what they learned was: "might makes right"; "the biggest kid in the sand box gets the shovel"; "I

win-you lose"; "you win, I lose"; or "you hurt me, I'll pay you back."

This is not to dismiss the mental health issues involved but these are the remedies that most often end at the barrel of a gun.

There are many causes of conflict at home, on the job and in the community. And individuals are unable to peacefully resolve them because no one has ever taught them how to peacefully resolve conflict.

We have some of the finest educational institutions in the world. However, few prepare students for the real world by teaching them the skills of how to address their own and others' emotions and to manage anger when dealing with conflict.

So what can we do? Obviously we can't re-educate every adult but we can take serious and meaningful steps to bring an end to this epidemic of gun violence.

Therefore I propose the following recommendation to simply to start the process to address the issues of mass killings

and gun violence:

• Conflict management as part of the school curriculum starting in kindergarten. If individuals learn to resolve, it is like learning to ride a bicycle or learning to swim. You never forget it.

• Establish a community mediation center. Individuals who are involved in a dispute will have a place to refer matters of interest and seek professional assistance.

• Encourage institutions and companies to establish a fair internal conflict-resolution process using alternative dispute resolution procedures.

• Demand that law enforcement recognize the importance of rights, restrictions, responsibility and respect.

• Establish more community mental health centers to address mental health issues.

• Implement Building Bridges Programs which will include diversity, culture competency and conflict resolution training.

Hezekiah Brown is a resident of Elizabeth City.

Teaching Black history could help defuse racism

HEZEKIAH BROWN

According to a new USA TODAY/Suffolk University poll, about 86% of respondents cited racism as a problem in the United States.

I firmly believe the way to alleviate this problem is for African American history to be incorporated into all levels of the American academic experience.

Appropriate level instruction recognizing the many valuable contributions to his country by African Americans would go far in alleviating the racism that exists today.

People who don't learn or study history are easily led and influenced to believe untruths. In other words, people who are not taught to analyze or draw conclusions from history are easily persuaded to view the world in an image crafted by another person.

Through no fault of their own most white Americans are ignorant of the many and important contributions that African Americans have made throughout this nation's history. For many, if they do think of black achievements they only think of entertainment and athletics.

According to a recent poll from Reuters, 40 percent of all white adults in America don't have any non-white friends. A report by the U.S. Department of Education released on June 7 confirms that public schools in the United States remain racially and socioeconomically segregated.

Almost 70 years after the U.S. Supreme Court outlawed "Separate but Equal" there are still places in the U.S. where students can go their entire educational careers without ever interacting with African Americans. This means that many school students have no personal experience to counter the negative messages they hear about African Americans. If all that children are ever taught about African Americans is what they see on television, in movies and on the news, they will have a skewed and negative view, which will affect how they treat African Americans and how they view the treatment of African Americans.

Learning about African American history allows students to have a deeper understanding and appreciation for the contributions of African Americans to the world we live in today. When students learn that African Americans have contributed positively to society, education, science, art, law and medicine, it gives them an appreciation for African Americans currently living in the United States.

It is the job of schools to teach children both factually correct information and how to think for themselves. Black history is needed to give students both the correct facts about African Americans and to teach them to think properly about the contributions of African Americans both historically and now. Teaching black history in schools will afford students who have little or no interaction with African Americans to develop an accurate understanding of them.

Today, as I observe states like Florida where politicians are banning books and passing legislation limiting education, I am reminded of some facts that have affected me. I attended segregated schools; walked past whites-only communities to get to the segregated Black High School; drank from segregated water fountains; rode standing in the back of the bus while there were "Whites Only" seats untaken in the front; watched the Ku Klux Klan burn crosses in the front of African American homes; and personally faced some form of discrimination on almost every job due to the color of my skin.

I have often asked myself and others, why are so many Americans be so hateful of other Americans? Why would they continue systemic racism and discrimination to a group of individuals who contributed so much to the cultural and economic success of this country?

Historically European Americans have enjoyed advantages in matters of education, immigration, voting rights, citizenship, land acquisition and criminal procedure. If 86% of Americans truly believe that racism is a problem, instead of purging libraries and banning books, adding African American history to the academic curriculums would go a long way toward resolution of the problem.

Hezekiah Brown, a retired federal mediator, is a resident of Camden, Delaware. He is a former resident of Elizabeth City.

Area labor leader eyed as state labor commissioner

HEZEKIAH BROWN, chairman of the state Mediation Board and a former Buffalo labor leader, is being mentioned as a strong candidate for the job of state labor commissioner.

Rumor has it that the current occupant of that post, Thomas F. Hartnett, may step down or be replaced in an administrative shuffle this summer.

The 52-year-old Brown, who makes his home on Long Island, learned about labor negotiations as a shop committeeman and later president of United Auto Workers Local 1173, representing workers at the former Chevrolet Tonawanda Foundry in the 1960s and early 1970s.

He became a federal mediator in 1972 in Buffalo before being transferred to the Federal Mediation and Conciliation Office in New York City.

State AFL-CIO President Edward Cleary says he may appoint a search committee to propose organized labor's choice for labor commissioner should the job become vacant.

Both Hartnett and Brown are popular with organized labor. So, too, is another rumored candidate for the po-

On The Job

By JOSEPH P. RITZ

sition, Barbara Patton, who heads the state Workers' Compensation Board.

The state's budget problems have increased speculation that the Mediation Board and the state Labor Relations Board will be merged, something that the state AFL-CIO opposes.

Hiring 'permanent' replacements can backfire on management

The use of "permanently" hired workers to replace strikers is a wet job that can backfire on the company use.

it. The most prominent examples are the Eastern Airline strike, in which the company went out of business, and Greyhound Bus Lines, which is operating under protection of a bankruptcy court. The results have been disastrous to both unions and management.

In the violence-marked New York Daily News strike, the owner, the Chicago Tribune Co., was forced to sell the paper, its circulation and advertising have not yet recovered and, at the conclusion of the strike, the replacements found that no one is over "permanently" hired. They were fired. That prompted the angry new employees hired to do the work of the striking pressmen to destroy part of the presses.

Even when the results are not so dramatic, a newly released study by the Economic Policy Institute reports that firms that have used permanent replacements during strikes had lower rates of production than companies that hired temporary replacements.

Firms that hired temporary employees during strikes operated at an average.

Hezekiah Brown worked at the Chevrolet Tonawanda Foundry plant.

See Labor Page A9

122

A young soldier in Little Rock

NEWSDAY PHOTO / KEN SPENCER

HEZEKIAH BROWN

Recalls helping
the Little Rock
Nine.

newsday.com/civilrights

Being born in segregated Prickett, Ala., inspired former Nassau Deputy County Executive Hezekiah Brown to succeed. On his way to high levels of local and state politics, Brown, 70, was a member of Gov. Mario Cuomo's cabinet, was a federal mediator and the youngest elected president of the United Auto Workers. But his journey began in the U.S. Army in 1957, when he was called to help the Little Rock Nine on their historic path.

■

"Once we arrived in Little Rock, Arkansas, we felt so good' . . . young, full of energy. . . . We thought that we were going to protect these black students. . . . All of a sudden, at the ripe old age of 18, I can now help fight this fight to help protect these students. . . . When we got there, they said all of the whites get off and the Negroes stay on the truck. I didn't hear that and I jumped off the truck. I was ready. . . . My sergeant said, 'Soldier get back on the truck.' . . . I followed orders and got back on the truck.

"That night . . . a group of young fellows . . . said this is our fight so we are going to go into town, we're going to march in, and we're going to take this fight on. . . . So I said, 'Look, guys, we are just not going to do this, because if we do, we are

'All of a sudden, at the ripe old age of 18, I can now help fight this fight to help protect these students.'

going to be shot down like dogs.' . . .

"While we all thought it was so wrong that African Americans did not go in to guard the students . . . in retrospect, it was the best thing that ever happened. . . . Because if we had been there, the school probably would never have been integrated because all the focus would have been on these young black guys who were not going to take anyone calling you names. . . . And we would have taken the fight on and all the focus would have been away from the Little Rock Nine."

— DEBORAH S. MORRIS

STATE
OF
NEW YORK

MARIO CUOMO
GOVERNOR

HEZEKIAH BROWN
CHAIRMAN

STATE MEDIATION BOARD

Hezekiah Brown – Chairman

George Sabatella – Board Member   Richard Torrey – Board Member

Dolores Whalen, Executive Secretary

MEDIATION SUPERVISORS

District	Supervisor	Address
Albany		Alfred E. Smith State Office Bldg., Albany, N.Y. 12225
Buffalo	Joseph Gentile	65 Court Street, Buffalo, N.Y. 14202
New York City	James McCabe	400 Broome Street, 10013
Syracuse	Charles Kaiser	State Office Bldg., Syracuse, NY 13202

STATE MEDIATORS

Eugene T. Coughlin   Joseph Lipowski
Roger A. Grothmann   Roger Maher
Mary Helenbrook   Joseph Pullano

BOARD MEMBERS

The Chairman of the State Mediation Board and the two Board Members are appointed by the Governor, with the advice and consent of the State Senate for a term of six years. Board members traditionally have been selected from the top levels of Industrial Relations, The Public Service, Law, Education, and Labor Relations. Board members are called upon by the Chairman to mediate difficult labor disputes. Their standing and prestige in the community, and with the parties are most helpful and effective in resolving difficult impasses. On occasion, members of the Board have been constituted as a mediation panel, and have acted jointly rather than individually to bring a dispute to a successful conclusion.

124

HEZEKIAH BROWN INDUCTED INTO THE NATIONAL ACADEMY OF ARBITRATORS

On MAY 24, 2008 AT THE ANNUAL MEETING OF THE NATIONAL ACADEMY OF ARBITRATORS WHICH WAS HELD IN OTTAWA, CANADA, FORMER HEMPSTEAD RESIDENT AND DEPUTY NASSAU COUNTY EXECUTIVE, HEZEKIAH BROWN WAS INDUCTED INTO THE NATIONAL ACADEMY OF ARBITRATORS.

THE NATIONAL ACADEMY OF ARBITRATORS IS A PROFESSIONAL AND HONORARY ORGANIZATION OF ARBITRATORS CHARGED WITH THE RESPONSIBILIY OF RESOLVING DISPUTES BETWEEN LABOR AND MANAGEMENT AND OTHERS

HEZEKIAH BROWN HAS BEEN INVOLVED IN THE ARBITRATION AND MEDIATION PROFESSION FOR OVER 35 YEARS WORKING AS A FEDERAL MEDIATOR AND CHIEF MEDIATOR FOR THE STATE OF NEW YORK UNDER GOVERNOR MARIO CUOMO. HE HAS ARBITRATED AND MEDIATED OVER 4000 LABOR-MANAGEMENT AND COMMUNITY DISPUTES INCLUDING SUCCESSFULLY MEDIATING THE DISPUTE BETWEEN THE HOTELS AND THE ELIZABETH CITY STATE UNIVERSITY NATIONAL ALUMNI ASSOCIATION./

THE NATIONAL ACADEMY OF ARBITRATORS IS A PROFESSIONAL AND HONORARY ORGANIZATION OF ARBITRATORS CHARGED WITH THE RESPONSIBILITY OF RESOLVING DISPUTES BETWEEN LABOR AND MANAGEMENT AND OTHERS.

THE PURPOSES FOR WHICH THE ACADEMY IS FORMED ARE:

TO ESTABLISH AND FOSTER THE HIGHEST STANDARDS OF INTEGRITY, COMPETENCE, HONOR AND CHARACTER AMONG THOSE ENGAGED IN THE ARBITRATION OF LABOR-MANAGEMENT DISPUTES ON A PROFESSIONAL BASIS.

TO SECURE THE ACCEPTANCE OF AND ADHERENCE TO THE CODE OF PROFESSIONAL RESPONSIBILITY FOR ARBITRATORS OF LABOR-MANAGEMENT DISPUTES PREPARED BY THE NATIONAL ACADEMY OF ARBITRATORS, THE AMERICAN ARBITRATION ASSOCIATION AND THE FEDERAL MEDIATION AND CONCILIATION SERVICE.

TO PROMOTE THE STUDY AND UNDERSTANDING OF THE ARBITRATION OF LABOR-MAMAGEMENT AND EMPLOYMENT DISPUTES:

TO ENCOURAGE FRIENDLY ASSOCIATION AMONG THE MEMBERS OF THE PROFESSIONAL; TO COOPERATE WITH OTHER ORGANIZATIONS, INSTITUTIONS AND LEARNED SOCIETIES INTERESTED IN LABOR-MANAGEMENT AND EMPLOYMENT RELATIONS, AND TO DO ANY AND ALL THINGS WHICH SHALL BE APPROPRIATE IN THE FUTHERANCE OF THESE PURPOSES.

Printed in the USA
CPSIA information can be obtained
at www.ICGtesting.com
CBHW060742070924
13930CB00009BA/99